# A BAND OF ARROGANT AND UNITED HEROES

Richard Pearson

# A BAND OF ARROGANT AND UNITED HEROES

The story of the Royal Shakespeare Company
production of

# THE WARS OF THE ROSES

**by**

**Richard Pearson**

**The Adelphi Press**
**4-6 Effie Road, London SW6 1TD**

Printed and Bound in U.K.
Typesetting by C.B.S. Felixstowe Suffolk IP11 7DR
Editors: Tom Deegan and Linda Lloyd
Published by Adelphi Press
ISBN 1 85654 005 7

For Maretta

The illustrations on the front cover are reproduced by kind permission of Donald Green, Mrs. Waldo Lanchester, Donald Burton and Piatnik of Vienna. Cover design by Jane Lashbrook.

**Photographs:** Gordon Goode, Geoffrey Wheeler, Dean Conger and John E. Fletcher © National Geographic Society, Stratford-upon-Avon Herald, Birmingham Post and Mail, and The Dirty Duck.

**Original Costume** designs by Ann Curtis, are gratefully reproduced with permission.

# ACKNOWLEDGEMENTS

I believe there are certain productions in the theatre which should not be allowed to diminish without record. This is contrary to a belief throughout the performing arts that it is the present that matters. But, perhaps every ten years, there comes a production so challenging and revelatory that its influence goes beyond the final curtain call.

In 1963, the production of 'The Wars of the Roses' at Stratford-upon-Avon established the Royal Shakespeare Company, presented a revolutionary style of design and introduced a number of exciting theatrical innovations.

This book tells of how the production was conceived, of the creative struggles through months of long rehearsals and of the performances which were received with overwhelming public and critical acclaim.

The story is told by the directors, designers, actors and production staff, and includes previously unpublished material. There has been no fabrication of events or creation of dialogue or opinion. Although twenty-six years have passed, the memories of those involved have remained as fresh as if it was yesterday.

The book is the result of a gathering together of material from many sources, and my grateful thanks are due to many individuals for their help and encouragement.

Sir Peter Hall's talks to the Company in April and July 1963 were recorded, and I am grateful to the Shakespeare Centre for granting access to them, and to Sir Peter for allowing me to use excerpts.

John Barton very kindly gave me the freedom of his extensive personal records of the production, which were a tremendous source in following the process of adaptation of the text, both before and during rehearsal.

Special thanks to those members of the "band of arrogant and united heroes" who shared their particular memories: Sir Peter Hall, John Barton, John Bury, Dame Peggy Ashcroft, John Corvin, Michael Craig, Ann Curtis, Jeffery Dench, Roy Dotrice, Susan Engel, Peter Geddis, Ian Holm, Martin Jenkins, Charles Kay, Brewster Mason, Cherry Morris, Clifford Rose, Nicholas Selby, Donald Sinden, Hugh Sullivan, Janet Suzman, David Warner, Guy Woolfenden; and for the contributions of others associated with the production: Donald Burton, Joe Clark, Brian Davenhall, Desmond Hall, Stephen Hancock, Roger Howells, Dorothy Marshall, J.M. McCloud, Colette O'Neil, Tim Pigott-Smith, Peter Pullinger, Michael Sarson, Ted Valentine, David Waller, Tony Watts and Chris Williams.

In addition, many others have helped in various ways: my friend Geoffrey Wheeler shared his enthusiasm and his large collection of photographs and critical material. Clifford Williams and Sir Len Hutton gave me their memories. The staffs of the Shakespeare Centre Library in Stratford-upon-Avon and the Shakespeare Library in the Birmingham City Library were unfailingly encouraging and helpful. Sally Beauman,

Bernard Levin and Robert Potter kindly gave permission to include extracts from their books and articles, and permission was given by Ariel Magazine, BBC Enterprises, Birmingham Post and Mail, Cambridge University Press, Coventry Evening Telegraph, The Guardian, Hodder and Stoughton, Manchester University Press, National Geographic Society, The Observer, Oxford University Press, Punch, Queen, Piatnik of Vienna, Routledge and Company, Stratford-upon-Avon Herald, The Sunday Times, The Times and William Kimber and Company to use copyright material.

I am grateful to John Barton and Ann Curtis who read the manuscript and, whilst suggesting a number of clarifications, provided additional memories.

My wife Maretta deserves special thanks for her understanding as our home acquired increasing numbers of heavy weapons and costumes, and her loving encouragement as the research for and writing of the story of 'The Wars of the Roses' took ever more of my time.

## FOREWORD:

## DAME PEGGY ASHCROFT

I was wondering how to begin this Foreword, when I read in the Independent on Sunday 6th January 1991, in a profile of Peter Hall by Irving Wardle, the following - "In 'The Wars of the Roses' he mounted the greatest Shakespearean event within living memory."

I don't know if my heart missed a beat or just went faster! But I hoped that many of my comrades from that "arrogant band" of those far-off days in 1963 and 1964 were also enjoying this tribute from one of our leading critics.

I won't say "it took me back" to those days because, of course, I had been re-living them in the pages of this book. Richard Pearson, the Holinshed of our "Wars" at Stratford, has recalled, through his minute research and with unabated enthusiasm, every detail of that event. It was indeed, for all of us who were part of the great adventure, something we shall never forget. Apart from its unique qualities as a production, it consolidated in those two years the inspiration of Peter's vision of a company, and was a living representation of what such a company could achieve. And this in the third year of its formation.

Apart from the production's own qualities, it had important results in the future work of the RSC. Those formerly thought to be "unpopular" plays - the three Henry VI's - became increasingly popular and took their place in the History Cycle performed in 1964. In 1977, Terry Hands directed three fascinating productions of the 'Henry VI's' in their entirety. And recently in "The Plantagenets", Adrian Noble used the Barton format - two plays in a contracted version of the three 'Henry's' plus Richard III - which had a tremendous success at Stratford and at the Barbican.

May I conclude this introduction with two personal anecdotes. I remember when Peter and John Barton first put the proposition of the trilogy to me I said, "I see, I suppose we shall be performing an all-day Shakespeare 'Oberammagau'!" "What a good idea!" they replied. I'm sure they would have decided to do this anyway, but it certainly set a precedent for all-day productions.

Finally a word on "The Roses ' cricket match - also included in this history! A cricket team - male of course - was traditional at Stratford, but in 1963 we achieved a match between the Houses of York and Lancaster led by Len Hutton and Cyril Washbrook, and including the reigning Queens of the two Houses. All in aid of World Freedom from Hunger. I would like to record my most treasured - if back-handed - compliment: Len Hutton saying to my son after the match (and my much boasted score of 16): "Well Nick, to see a woman of your mother's age put on pads and run like that is a bloody marvel!"

My ever grateful thanks to Peter Hall, John Barton and the Company; to Len Hutton and Cyril Washbrook and above all to our immortaliser, Richard Pearson.

## FOREWORD:

## SIR PETER HALL

''Richard Pearson's anthology of memories of THE WARS OF THE ROSES has jerked me back to the obsessions, pains and pleasures of nearly thirty years ago. The book is a friendly and generous commemoration of a great deal of hard work and excitement. For me personally, it was both a wonderful and a terrible time. My over-riding feeling in reading this book is that I was a very lucky young man, blessed in my colleagues. First, I was lucky to be championed by Sir Fordham Flower - ''Fordie'', the chairman of the Stratford board. He was a visionary, and I owed much to him. He backed my visions and stuck by me through thick and thin. And without the Company there would have been no WARS OF THE ROSES.

There are of course many others and they are lauded in these pages: Peggy Ashcroft, genius actress and staunch friend who led the Company; John Barton, collaborator and provoker extraordinary; Peter Brook, who truly performed the office of a friend and, when doctors forbade me to work for six months, told me to get back into the saddle immediately; John Bury, a great designer; and above all the Company - a band of great and dedicated actors, musicians and technicians, who supported and inspired me on this arduous journey.

I am usually very glad that the theatre is ephemeral - for true theatre is only of its own time, and has to be. But it is good to know now that a tape of THE WARS OF THE ROSES still exists at Stratford in the flickering black and white of the 1960's television. It had been thought that the BBC archives had destroyed it in order to make new room on its shelves. But one copy remains and the shadows are a tribute to the efforts of this great Company.

I still think that politics is an inescapably dirty business. I still think simulation and hypocrisy are indispensable talents for any politician. I still think that Shakespeare showed shrewdly and compassionately the dangers and the corruption of power. Public accountability and true freedom of speech will always be the only safeguard for any country.

Shakespeare, I am sure, would well understand the problems of the present. A modern democracy needs ambitious people to run it. But they must be curbed and checked, otherwise their ambitions will ruin the very ideals they are trying to serve. THE WARS OF THE ROSES still has a lesson.''

## LIST OF ILLUSTRATIONS AND PHOTOGRAPHS

# THE WARS OF THE ROSES

# CHAPTER ONE

"All these people, all their memories; there's a book here waiting to be written," said Guy Woolfenden, the Head of Music for the Royal Shakespeare Company.

It was at the Tredington Mill Gallery in July 1987, where an exhibition commemorated the RSC's production of 'The Wars of the Roses'.

Crowded into a room behind the exhibition area, a group of actors, designers, musicians, dressmakers and stage managers watched a brief piece of 8mm film of 'Henry VI'. As the grey images appeared on the white wall, members of the group cried out in joyful recognition of the scene before them, and Guy Woolfenden hummed choruses of the music he had composed.

That day there was great pride in being part of what Peter Brook had called "a vast and rich achievement".

The cycle of three plays opened to overwhelming critical and public acclaim in July and August 1963. Audiences were in turn confronted, challenged and captivated by Peter Hall's vision. As he had always hoped, and indeed intended when he decided to present the plays, the powerful images spoke directly for that time.

"He was deeply concerned with what he believed was the overall conception of the plays," Dame Peggy Ashcroft has said. "Peter was very much interested in the political aspects of the plays, and in 'The Wars of the Roses' there was *so* much that was political."

"It was a horrific analysis of power politics," wrote the critic of 'Plays and Players'.

"You could see the power machine, the emphasis on the throne, on the crown, on the conference table... All that was so beautifully explicit," considered John Kane, who was a young member of the 1964 company when the production was re-staged.

The production *was* revolutionary. "A watershed in Theatre," believes Janet Suzman; "the most influential single event of those years...the pinnacle of the RSC's achievement," thinks Ian Richardson.

For Roy Dotrice, its effect spread widely: "It was recognisable in theatre companies all over the country. The way actors spoke, the groupings, and the set and costume materials."

John Bury, who designed the production, and Ann Curtis, who collaborated with him on the costumes, still recognise 'Wars of the Roses' imagery and textures in opera and theatre throughout the world.

What made the production exceptional were the actors - and not just any actors but *those* actors, producing, in Peter Hall's judgement, "the extraordinary power of special people." The establishment of a company of actors, working together continuously on a repertory of Shakespeare at Stratford and a mixture of new and classic plays at a

London theatre, had been the basis of Peter Hall's thinking when he took control of the Shakespeare Memorial Theatre in 1960. By the Spring of 1963, when rehearsals for 'The Wars of the Roses' began, the Company was composed of actors who had worked together for several seasons, and had become well versed and tirelessly trained in Peter Hall's approach to the delivery of Shakespearean text - a delivery which he believed had to be "cool, unsentimental and unromantic." In addition, a number of actors were brought into the Company, whose experience and personality would assist the epic sweep of the plays which was Hall's chief interest.

It was unintentional that the 22-year-old David Warner, cast as Henry VI, would become a star and create an international sensation with his performance. In fact, Hall had taken a great gamble in casting the unknown Warner to play against Dame Peggy Ashcroft as Queen Margaret.

A number of actors in the Company received wider recognition, especially after the Quatercentenary celebrations in 1964 and the televising of 'The Wars of the Roses' in 1965, in both this country and the United States. Roy Dotrice, Ian Holm, Janet Suzman and Eric Porter, like David Warner, subsequently moved into television and films.

In 1963, Peter Hall at 32 and his friend John Barton, who was 33, were two of the 'Young Turks' who were influencing the direction of theatre at that time. Absolutely dedicated to a world of experiment, Hall had told the members of the Royal Shakespeare Company at the beginning of the year: "The whole thing - stage, setting, costumes, speaking, creative acting - is all in a state of finding; of not expecting final solutions, but keeping open." He challenged convention and rejected conformity.

"A gambler and a politician," said Ian Holm, "and a hard man to get to know. Yet there was something about him - I don't know what - that attracted your loyalty."

Nicholas Selby thought Hall "a consummate politician. He would smile at you and convince you that what he wanted was what you wanted, whilst at the same time slipping a stiletto blade into you."

"I watched him once listening to a heated discussion between John Bury and John Barton," recalls Ann Curtis. "They were challenging each other with creative ideas, and Peter just sat, saying nothing but hearing everything. He was selecting the best of the ideas."

'The Wars of the Roses' was an adaptation of the three parts of Henry VI plus Richard III. John Barton cut and transposed the plays and, in addition, wrote original lines based on the Chronicles of Holinshed. The first play, 'Henry VI', covered the period from the funeral of Henry V to the deaths of Gloucester and Winchester and the murder of Suffolk. The second, called 'Edward IV', continued the story from Jack Cade's rebellion to Margaret's defeat at Tewkesbury and the murder of Henry VI. The third, 'Richard III', brought the Wars to their conclusion, and contained a number of new lines to link the earlier plays.

John Barton constructed the adaptation, which underwent several revisions during rehearsals in 1963 and when the plays were re-staged in 1964. It remained a living text, with Barton's fertile creativity suggesting new passages and responding to the re-working of a scene or the re-interpretation of a character.

Roy Dotrice called it "John Barton's juggling act. He had a large board with scraps of paper, on which he had written odd lines, pinned to it. And he would move them about, adding new ones, discarding others."

"With 'The Wars of the Roses', Peter Hall challenged everything," said Brewster Mason. "You must remember that it was 1963. Theatres didn't adapt and re-write Shakespeare plays. Theatres didn't present three plays in one day. But he did."

The story of the Royal Shakespeare Company's production of 'The Wars of the Roses' centres on the driving force of Peter Hall, his inspiration and determination to present a political and theatrical experience, reinforcing his conviction that Shakespeare's expression of the human condition has a timely lesson and a modern relevance.

# CHAPTER TWO

It is likely, though not certain, that Shakespeare wrote the First Part of 'Henry VI' in 1591 when he was 28. For in March of the following year a performance of a new play called 'Harey the VI' was recorded in the "Diary" of Philip Henslowe. Apparently this First Part was popular, for it led to the appearance of Parts Two and Three by the Summer of 1592. However, even this is surmised and there is conjecture that the Second and Third Parts of 'Henry VI' may even have been written before Part One.

Even with these cloudy origins, the plays were a success with the public, and versions of Parts Two and Three were printed in 1594 and 1595 respectively. These Quartos were reprinted in 1600 and once again - this time as one play - in 1619.

Although attributed to Shakespeare, the actual authorship of the Three Parts of 'Henry VI' has engaged scholars in digging and guesswork for centuries, and the speculation is both stimulating and fascinating. Part One is the most questionable and uneven of the three, with much pot-boiling rhetoric. Whilst Parts Two and Three contain a mass of dramatic deadwood, clichés and inconsistencies.

Several sixteenth century contemporaries of Shakespeare have been suggested as collaborators - Robert Greene, George Peele, Thomas Nashe, Thomas Kyd and Christopher Marlowe - with Shakespeare's contribution that of reviser.

The sources of the plays are clearer and identifiable. Indeed, many of the passages in 'Henry VI' sit side by side with the source books which Shakespeare used. Each of the historians wrote his Chronicle during the reign of Henry VII, because he won. At the very best, it should make us cautiously aware of the colour of the interpretation.

Henry VII commissioned an Italian humanist, Polydore Vergil, to write an official history of England. Vergil's book was the foundation of a lively tradition of Tudor historiography and propaganda, culminating in the two works that were Shakespeare's principal source of information for the 'Henry VI' plays: Edward Hall's 'The Union of the Two Noble and Illustre Families of Lancaster and York' published in 1548, and Raphael Holinshed's 'The Chronicles of England, Ireland and Scotland' published in 1578 - Shakespeare referred to the second edition of 1587. The belief that Henry VII was the 'Saviour of England' is basic to all three books. Also, Shakespeare appears to have drawn on Richard Fabyan's 'Chronicle', Geoffrey of Monmouth's 'Historia Regum Britanniae', Foxe's 'Acts and Monuments' and 'A Mirror For Magistrates', a Tudor collection of historical poems.

The historian C.T. Allmand wrote that in his book, Vergil had shown how the events of the fifteenth century followed an almost inevitable pattern, in which justice had to be seen to be done. After the deposition of Richard II there was an inexorable path to further deposition. Herschel Baker considered that, like the Book of Genesis and the Aeneid, Hall's 'Union' told the story of a people that, under divine guidance, fulfilled its destiny. Furthermore, "Hall had a double purpose: to expound the providential theme that 'as by discord great things decay and fall to ruin, so the same by concord be revived and erected', and to celebrate the glories of the Tudors. Like many other writers of his age, Hall considered politics to be a branch of morals."

The sweep of these books was an inspiration to Shakespeare, and it is easy to appreciate how the patriotic fervour captured the imagination of the young playwright. Skill and audacity were required to tell the vast canvas of fifty years of frenetic English history. Sometimes the writing is raw and unpolished, but sometimes it soars magnificently.

Herschel Baker considered that to mould so great a theme required a shaping hand, and cautioned that the plays in no way really describe what happened in the fifteenth century. Shakespeare manipulated, fabricated, telescoped, distorted and rearranged to reinforce his own interpretation of things found in Hall and Holinshed. C.T. Allmand's view was that, having decided upon the overall nature of his theme, Shakespeare fitted and moulded his characters to suit his purposes. And, since the theme itself is dark and tragic, many of the figures share these characteristics.

The theme was big. The Houses of York and Lancaster were derived from two lines of descent from Edward III. Edward was succeeded by his grandson Richard II. Richard, who had no children, was deposed in 1399, the crown went to Henry IV and passed directly to his son and grandson Henry V and Henry VI. Henry VI was descended from John of Gaunt, Duke of Lancaster, who was the fourth son of Edward III.

Henry IV had stepped over the heads of another line of claimants, the Mortimers and the Earls of March, because they were descended from the third son of Edward III, Lionel Duke of Clarence. It was his daughter, Anne Mortimer, who married into yet another branch of the family and was the mother of Richard Plantagenet, the Duke of York who appears in 'Henry VI'. That was the essence of the Yorkist case, namely, that when Henry IV took the throne, the line of succession had taken a wrong turning, and should therefore be restored to those in the rightful line of descent.

Shakespeare carried this theme through the three plays and, explained very simply, Part One is about the ambitions of the English nobles who fight amongst themselves for the power which King Henry VI is too ineffectual to use, and they eventually unite into rival packs. Part Two is entirely about the ruthless civil strife during the Wars of the Roses, between groups of those great nobles who are members of families close to the King. In Part Three, Henry is deposed by the Duke of York and, after York's death, his sons fight on. Finally, Henry is murdered by Richard of Gloucester, who later becomes Richard III. It must be said that, theatrically, the separate plays do not stand happily by themselves, but seen together in sequence their force is exciting and rich.

Therefore, somewhat paradoxically, following its successful opening at Philip Henslowe's Rose Theatre in 1592, the First Part of Henry VI - or a version of it - and the subsequent Parts Two and Three, received few performances over the following centuries. Perhaps the Elizabethan audiences found the plays relevant, particularly as their grandparents had lived through the actual events. However, during the seventeenth and eighteenth centuries the plays were performed infrequently, and then only in versions very far removed from Shakespeare's texts and bearing little relation to the originals.

In 1681, John Crowne, drawing on the second and third parts of Shakespeare's 'Henry VI' and adding a few bits of his own, had little success presenting 'Henry VI, with the Murder of Humphrey of Gloucester' and 'The Misery of Civil War'. Forty-two years later, Ambrose Philip used little over thirty-five lines from 'Henry VI Part Two' for 'Humphrey Duke of Gloucester'. The chief interest of this production was the playing of Cardinal Beaufort by Colley Cibber. In the same year, 1723, 'An Historical Tragedy of the Civil Wars in the Reign of King Henry 6th' lasted one performance. Theophilus Cibber borrowed from Shakespeare and John Crowne, added lines of his own and even some lines from 'Henry V'.

In the eighteenth century, one performance of the original 'Henry VI Part One' was given at Covent Garden in 1738. Other than that, the plays were neglected.

Preference for adaptation was revived in the nineteenth century. In 1817, John Herman Merivale drew almost entirely from Part Two for 'Richard, Duke of York, or The Contention of York and Lancaster', in which Edmund Kean played York. Despite critics, it played for seven performances.

The first Stratford production of 'Henry VI Part 1' came at the end of the nineteenth century, with Osmond Tearle using properties and costumes borrowed from Henry Irving. In 1906, Frank Benson, Director of the old Memorial Theatre, mounted all three parts on consecutive evenings, and played both Talbot and Richard of Gloucester.

In the 1920s, Robert Atkins staged the trilogy at the Old Vic, but no-one observed, or perhaps even knew, that it was the very first London production for three hundred years of the three plays as Shakespeare had written them.

Finally, there was a celebrated presentation of the trilogy by the Birmingham Repertory Theatre, first with 'Henry VI Part Two', in April 1951, Part Three in April 1952, and then Part One in June 1953. Directed by Douglas Searle and using an amplified text by Sir Barry Jackson, they were performed in chronological order later that year at the Old VIc. Four years later they were remounted, with much success, once again at the Old Vic. These were the productions seen by both Peter Hall and John Barton.

In spite of the flurry of attention during the first half of this century, the plays, their characters and their stories remained very largely unknown. They occupied that place in the public awareness reserved for the so-called 'unpopular' plays by Shakespeare: 'King John', 'Titus Andronicus' and 'Timon of Athens'. Perhaps the public recalled the events from a contact in history lessons at school, or perhaps at the time of the annual country cricket match between Yorkshire and Lancashire. Even the term 'The

Wars of the Roses' was not Shakespeare's, but believed to have been created by Sir Walter Scott. Maybe the problem was that, although the plays contained some beautiful and stirring passages, none of them appeared in the anthologies.

It was their perceptive analysis of power and the corruption of politicians that first attracted Peter Hall to the plays, whilst a student at Cambridge in 1950. He was fascinated and intrigued, but never thought that they would concern him as a director, for in those days, as Hall recalls, "I was more interested in the revelation of human character in drama than in the expression of social or political images."

For his friend and fellow Cambridge student, John Barton, the appeal was stronger, and he "dreamed of a definitive production of the 'Henry VI's'."

When Peter Hall became Director of the Stratford Memorial Theatre in 1960, he asked John Barton to join him. High on their list of projects were the 'Henry VI' plays, but still "I was not attracted to the plays myself." Hall approached Peter Brook with the invitation to direct the plays, but Brook was not interested and refused. When Brook became part of the directoral triumvirate in 1962, Hall asked him again. Again Brook declined, but this time suggested that Hall himself should direct them.

"I felt a growing awareness of the significance of politics. I suddenly realised that it's not power that corrupts, but that you have to corrupt yourself to be politically powerful. Shakespeare knew that too. It was buried in the plays," Peter Hall remembers. "I had always thought of them being done, but never really considered taking on the job myself."

As a result, Hall admitted, the plays rapidly grew into an obsession. What he called "developments in my own understanding" helped the decision.

First, "Shakespeare believed that there was a natural order in nature, starting with the lowest forms of life and moving up through the beasts to man and to God. All Shakespeare's thinking, whether religious, political or moral, is based on a complete acceptance of this concept of order. There is a just proportion in all things: man is above beast, king is above man and God above king. Revolution, whether in the individual's temperament, in the family or in the state or in the heavens, destroys the order and leads to destructive anarchy. Even if this chaos is inevitable and necessary, it is still a sin, and punishment will follow the violation of natural laws."

So, in deposing Richard II, Henry Bolingbroke and his family suffered retribution for generations.

"It is wrong to depose a king, just as it is wrong for the heart to rule the head, or for any extremes in persons or politics to be victorious. Man must therefore govern himself with the care of an army or a state:

'Take but degree away, untune that string,
And hark what discord follows'."

Hall never felt there was much life in the theory that there is a difference between learning and understanding. "But as I worked year in and year out on Shakespeare I began to see it, not as a relic of medievalism but as a piece of workable human pragmatism, humanitarian in its philosophy and modern and liberal in its application."

There was also Peter Hall's acute and personal interest in politics.

"Over the years I became more and more fascinated by the contortions of politicians, and by the corrupting seductions experienced by anybody who wields power. I began to collect 'sanctions' - those justifications which politicians use in the press and on television to mask the dictates of their party politics or their personal ambitions: 'not in the public interest'; 'the country is not ready for it'; 'the man in the street will never accept' ... I realised that Shakespeare's history plays were full of such sanctions: 'God', 'Fortune', 'The Common Weal', 'Duty', 'St. George', 'England', 'France'. What had seemed conventional rhetoric was really, when spoken by Warwick or Richard III, an ironic revelation of the time-honoured practices of politicians. I realised that the mechanisms of power had not changed in centuries. We also were in the middle of a blood-soaked century. I was convinced that a presentation of one of the bloodiest and most hypocritical periods in history would teach many lessons about the present."

The plan to present the 'Henry VI' plays was a bold one, and made even more exciting by the decision to add 'Richard III' in order to capture the full sweep of the retributory theme. They further believed that Richard III "would emerge as a different, richer play." The timing of the decision was also particularly daring and was characteristic of Peter Hall's dash and élan.

The 'Henry VI' plays were very much box-office uncertainties, and would be a great gamble because, in 1962, Hall's Royal Shakespeare Company was under "intense pressure" and "engaged in what was extensively publicised as a battle for survival ... unremitting and impassioned". The Company's financial resources were near exhaustion and applications for state subsidy had received a frosty response. But Peter Hall's impetuous personality was his greatest strength in difficult situations, and he enjoyed taking risks.

When he was appointed Director of the Shakespeare Memorial Theatre in 1960, he announced plans of great adventure and panache: to establish a Company of contracted artists who would work together over a long period; to secure a theatre in London to which Stratford productions could transfer and where modern and classic plays could be presented to complement and enlighten their Shakespeare work. At the end of the 1960 season, Hall established his Company's London base at the Aldwych Theatre.

There were triumphs and disappointments, but they were times of creativity, imagination and great drive. Roy Dotrice remembers them also as happy family times. Their babies were christened in Shakespeare's church and their older children attended the local schools. They lived first along with other Company families, including Ian Holm's, at Avoncliffe - an attractive Georgian-style house and the home of Leslie Caron and Peter Hall - beside the Avon at Tiddington, and later in their own home at Tredington - which became quite a Company corner when John Bury and Brewster

Mason moved to the village. There were Company picnics at Alveston, and Roy tried, unsuccessfully, to build a Company baseball team, similar to the one he had gathered during the 1959 season, which had included Paul Robeson, Albert Finney, Sam Wanamaker, Laurence Olivier and Charles Laughton. Avoncliffe became the central point of all Stratford theatre activity, with parties on the lawns and regular Company gatherings. The delightful old house, with its stables, outhouses and lovely conservatory, was demolished in 1971. Only the tall, red-brick wall remains.

They were exciting years, as Hall drove himself and his Company - from 1961 named the Royal Shakespeare Company. He explained that his policy was to express the richness of Shakespeare so that it became immediate to modern audiences and offered the actors "the chance to be part of a strong Company, producing revolutionary work." Young actors were attracted by the increasingly democratic, anti-hierarchic structure and the opportunity for rapid promotion to major parts if their talent showed. "Hall was offering idealism."

The régime was indeed almost puritanical. Peter Hall himself worked 17-hour days. Techniques had to be learnt and developed until Shakespeare's form became a discipline, supporting rather than denying self-expression.

The actors were taught where the line endings were, they had to find an emotional reason for the shape of the text, they had to know where the punctuation was operating, what it was doing, where the half lines were, so that they took a cue on the half line. And everything had to scan. Peter Hall called it "learning the score". Once they had learned it they could start thinking about being real.

This was all part of artistic security, and Hall wrote that in it lay "the Company's strength."

Nevertheless, Hall later realised that "the common spirit of a Company which had been created by the end of 1960 had disintegrated" the following year, and it was not until the return of many of the 1960 Company to Stratford in 1962, and the successful experiences from the nourishing work with the Arts Theatre season in the same year, that a strong Company spirit was regained.

It was a "key year in the development of the Royal Shakespeare Company" and "the moment when it found the style that was to characterise its best work under Hall's directorship". The Company staged twenty-four productions and the extent of its work, coinciding with its fight for survival, had "a galvanic effect." Peter Hall was able to assert: "The Company is beginning to form a definite personality ... the spirit remains youthful, pragmatic and forward-looking."

The decision to present the tetralogy did not receive unanimous support amongst the RSC's administration, nor were there many who shared his enthusiasm. Some considered it folly to do the plays at a time when the Company's fortunes were so precarious. But Hall had the intuitive conviction that the plays, though diffuse and uneven in quality as they stood, would, when cut and condensed, speak with great relevance to their modern audience. So his brief to John Barton was to turn three plays into two. Specifically: to streamline, to focus and to sharpen.

The years of "brooding" about "a definitive production of gangster power politics" were over. They had hatched the plan together, knew each other's minds, understood each other's intentions. In John Barton, Peter Hall had "a colleague who combined the affinities of a friend, the erudition of a scholar, the talent of a director and the mystery of an eminence grise."

John Barton read English at King's College, Cambridge from 1949, and the two influences upon him, to a greater and lesser extent, were apparently George Rylands and Muriel Bradbrook. Rylands' book 'Words and Poetry' promoted "the practical values of translating Shakespeare's words on the page to a life on the stage" and Bradbrook's 'Elizabethan Stage Conditions: A Study of their place in the interpretation of Shakespeare's plays' stressed that the "young scholar-directors know the conditions and conventions of playing before tackling the content of Shakespeare's dramas".

Of Rylands, John Barton has said: "I think ... his insistence on verse speaking made me very aware of it. He enormously stimulated me ..."

Barton immersed himself in the many student-run domestic societies, and "is best remembered at Cambridge as a director of imagination, insight, and some daring".

It has been said that during his Cambridge years, Barton nurtured two ambitions. One was for definitive Shakespeare productions and the other was "a passion to be a playwright". Indeed, he wrote three plays, whilst his theatrical activities were quite prodigious: acting in more than forty productions, directing many others and influencing many more. With George Rylands he co-directed a 'Romeo and Juliet', playing Mercutio with Peter Hall as Tybalt. His hugely successful production of 'Julius Caesar' used what was believed to have been the Elizabethan dialect. As co-founder of the Oxford-Cambridge Players, which later became the Elizabethan Theatre Company, he directed 'Henry V', which was televised by the BBC in 1953 and toured during that year.

Barton joined the Drama Department of the University of California at Berkeley in the Autumn of 1953 to lecture on English Renaissance drama, and then returned to Cambridge the following year on a Fellowship to research modern drama. In 1956 he was appointed Lay Dean of King's College and began a very productive period, developing his work on Early English drama and with the Marlowe Society.

When Peter Hall invited John Barton to Stratford as Assistant Director "to teach the actors of his new Company to speak the verse as (both of them) had learned from Rylands, Barton was 'delighted' ... to take up Hall's challenge". For the 1960 Stratford season, Hall assigned 'The Taming of the Shrew' to Barton. Weeks before the opening, members of the cast (including Dame Peggy Ashcroft) approached Peter Hall with "grievances concerning Barton's directorial methods", claiming that "he climbed over them".

Hall took over the production and asked Barton to leave, but he refused, later recalling that "I doggedly stuck it out and hung on ... because I felt all would sort itself out."

Roy Dotrice remembers, "After 'The Shrew', John was often found wandering disconsolately in the corridors."

So Barton devoted himself to teaching verse and acting classes, directed 'Carmen' at Sadler's Wells, wrote the very successful anthology 'The Hollow Crown' and "waited for the call which he felt would one day come".

Whilst appearing in 'The Hollow Crown' in New York in 1963 he received the call.

During 1962 he and Peter Hall had discussed ideas for a production of 'Henry VI' and 'Richard III' and, by December, John had completed a first draft before leaving for America. Now he was asked to return to England to complete major revisions of the text.

John's original brief was "only to cut and condense the plays drastically". But there was a further consideration. "We wanted to play them as part of a cycle culminating with 'Richard III'. In addition, in order to interest audiences in the plays as a single entity, we decided to use the overall title of 'The Wars of the Roses', and on occasion to play the whole cycle on a single day.

"Consequently one of my main tasks was to cut the texts to fit the playing time available."

He summarised his action with the first draft. "In order to combine the plays, I had to do a version. I had to reword the text in some way. Now at the outset, Peter and myself had no intention of reworking or rewriting the text.

"What happened was that when I put together Shakespeare's Part One with the first half of Part Two, and the second half of Part Two with his Part Three, I found that we actually had two unhandable objects because, crude though these plays were, they did have some sort of ending. But where I had divided them, they didn't quite hold together dramatically."

This was a problem. They had to bear in mind that people were going to see perhaps one of these plays, and that each one, though part of a cycle, had also to be self-sufficient.

"It was at that moment that we decided to adapt further than our initial intention."

John Barton reasoned at the outset that, because of the playing time available, "It was clear that many passages would have to go which, in other circumstances, we would certainly have kept." He soon discovered that normal linear cutting still left the plays too long. "As each of the plays is longer than many in the canon, this meant in practical terms that a total of over 12,350 lines had to be reduced to half this number."

This presented Barton with new problems, for with cutting, "Inconsistencies in the plot became more noticeable."

It was quickly evident that "clarifying passages were needed for shifts in time and locality, and clarification of character titles, alternames and relationships of characters unfamiliar to audiences unversed in English history."

This was necessary "not only to compress a mass of confusing incidents, but in order to clarify Shakespeare's vision of the forging of England". John had to preserve Shakespeare's double vision - "plain enough even in these early works - of life as an evolving process and as a meaningless jangle, of kings as tyrants and as tired men, of the common people as both suffering human beings and as an insensate mob".

The problem was paramount with their 'Henry VI' which, after the initial cutting, remained "shapeless". Barton considered its two failings: "It builds to no climax ... The characters have no complexity or development." There were other points that troubled him, and these were detailed in an illuminating exchange of memoranda with Peter Hall:

*John Barton:* "What is 'Henry VI' about? And what are its main themes? The central action concerns Henry's relationship with Gloucester and their ultimate failure to help one another. He tried to make a King of Henry, and when Henry does act for himself it is always against Gloucester. He marries against Gloucester's advice, removes him from office and, misled by Margaret and Suffolk, makes the mistake of believing that Gloucester himself is the chief obstacle to his establishing himself as King. He allows himself to be persuaded that Gloucester is a secret traitor, but in the final scene of the play Winchester's death-bed confession opens his eyes. The confession should establish one of the main moral points in the trilogy: namely, that self-seeking and wickedness breed guilt in the doer and rejection by other people. More important, it should beget an enormous guilt in Henry, and the play should end with his appalled acceptance of the fact that his weakness has been responsible for the death of Gloucester.

"The lack of depth, development or interplay of character among the principals is particularly worrying as far as the character of the King himself is concerned. His saintliness is only a label, and his weakness an uninteresting fact. He would become more interesting if we gave him a definite line of development throughout the play. At the outset he is naive and benevolent, but unconfident. He leans enormously on Gloucester and Winchester. Later, Gloucester goads him into trying to stand on his own feet, and the only occasion on which he does so is when he marries Margaret against Gloucester's advice. The rest of the time he opts out with pious sentiments. Gloucester's murder finally goads him into a positive, concrete, morally-motivated action - the banishment of Suffolk. But this turns the Queen against him, and her destructive nature spends itself in destroying him."

In his response, Peter Hall agreed on the need for radical action.

"We certainly need Winchester's death-bed confession making the main moral point that self-seeking and wickedness breed guilt in the doer and rejection by other people, and I like your idea very much that this should make Henry guiltily aware that his weakness has been responsible for the death of Gloucester. My basic feeling is that we need to pare down the inessentials, clarify the plot line and have fewer scenes.

"I think we need to hammer home throughout the play, in order to make it acceptable at all, the concept of order as a living, changing thing, both in the individual and in the state. Men and countries must be open to a rational equilibrium produced by all the forces working on them in order to be natural, virtuous and moral. You said to me once that you thought we should cut down the amount of railing Gloucester does; I believe this to be wrong. The turbulent, self-destructive temper that this very virtuous man has is a perfect theme in the play. He is nearly ordered, but not quite."

*John Barton:* "There is an important point (about Margaret's development) not clearly defined in (the original text). This could give humanity and background to her scolding - the effect on her of marriage to a weak and sexually unsatisfying husband. If we can show her disillusionment in this respect more clearly in our 'Henry VI', it will lead naturally to her sublimation of his failure in her private life when she becomes an Amazon in the field in the latter part of (the second play).

"The hurt wrought by her contempt for (the King) is not placed in the original play: it would be an enormous help dramatically if it could be included in the revised version. It would show that he uses his monkish pre-disposition as a defence mechanism, although he knows at bottom that he is abusing his moral sense in order to evade responsibility."

*Peter Hall:* "I am not sure that you should stress that Henry was deeply in love with Margaret. I think he hoped and thought that she would give him the help and confidence he needed, and if she had he would have found love, respect and security. But I think mainly he is governed by what he thinks he ought to do - he *ought* to be a firm King. He *ought* to be fair. He *ought* to be a husband. He *ought* to be a father. He *ought* to make this marriage."

*John Barton:* "I think we can also cut down the personal brawling a good deal further, and should get away from baronial rhodomontade by using the council-table as much as possible: meetings may always break up in disorder, but they should start formally with a concrete agenda to be tackled. The Council is the centre of government and at its meetings each of the various vaunting lords is trying to impose his will on his colleagues.

"I wonder if it wouldn't help to lose most of the bickering between Gloucester and Winchester and present it instead as Henry's first Council Meeting, a meeting at which everybody tries to behave well and the cracks in the fabric are only hinted at."

This introduction was a very major factor in the entire cycle, and it became a major cross-reference intended to heighten the political themes of the plays that fascinated Peter Hall and John Barton. It was an inspiration and came from one of Barton's subjective and creative urges. He said later, "The introduction of the Council Board and the King's Council as a formal point was the biggest insert, the biggest addition we made. No doubt about it." It was also a key production point, "more obvious in the theatre than in the text itself. As one by one the barons were uprooted, so the Council's membership changed".

Later the critic Bamber Gascoigne considered, "The central theme of the play is the black strategy of the Council Table, a fascinating X-ray of a struggle for power, which turns out to be Barton's rather than Shakespeare's."

As the pressure increased with the approach of the first rehearsal in April, Barton began the ruthless cutting and slashing of the text with urgency. He worked from eight in the morning in his study overlooking New Cavendish Street in London. Meanwhile, Peter Hall was busy re-staging his production of 'A Midsummer Night's Dream' at the Aldwych Theatre. Each evening they met either at John's home or at Hall's in Montpellier Square, and far into the night discussed Barton's revision. They were sweeping. Sixty characters disappeared, including the Countess of Auvergue, the Earl of Salisbury, the Marquess of Montague and the Mortimers.

Much later, Roy Dotrice mused, "John had done a marvellous job of trimming and cutting the fifteen Dukes of Wigan, St.Helens and Crewe!"

And Donald Sinden remembers that "he concertina'ed certain events to clarify the narrative line and, when he found that the jagged ends left by his cuts failed to join satisfactorily, the amazing Barton ... was not above writing new lines of blank verse".

An understatement. Barton had already been writing linking passages, based on Shakespeare or Holinshed, but it had become clear to both of them that the surgery would have to be far more radical.

The results were indeed amazing. The revisions needed whole new passages, transpositions and telescoping.

"We did not attempt to ape Shakespeare's style, but to fill out what we took to be his thematic thinking." Hall remembers that Barton "could soon turn out early Shakespearean verse that could fool any expert".

John Barton's memory is that "re-writing was not too hard. Once you got into the swing of the style and made sure the grammar and words you used were current in Shakespeare's time, the problem was knowing when to stop".

A point stressed by Peter Hall. "He did it so well that, if he hadn't been checked, we'd have ended up with something simply 'based on a play by William Shakespeare'."

Dame Peggy Ashcroft recalls: "There were certain passages when John got carried away, and these were eliminated from the final text. There was one magnificent death scene."

Many others of the cast remember it too. It was Winchester's in the final scene of

'Henry VI'.

Peter Hall has said, "It was so perfectly in spirit with the 'Henry VI's' that our publicity department, having only read an early draft of the text, included it in the proof copy of a programme as a fine piece of typical early Shakespeare."

"What is a man? Proud Warwick, know thy kind?
A man's a dog, and dogs do crave a master,
For what's a dog but a half-tamed wolf?
And who should do that office? Who should tame him?
Who keep the curs in kennel? Why, a king;
And what's his state but such a kind of kennel
Where he can best contain their savagery?
How should he rule? Why, fill their bellies up,
Shift straw, tent scabs, scour worms, anoint their tetters,
Bathe them with herb o'grace when they breed lice,
And whip them well betimes. Is that not kingly?
A king's no dog; a king's a braver beast:
Methinks he is a lion, or should be so,
For you and I were hounds to such a master.
But now we have a lamb, a silly lamb,
That when we bark, he bleats; and when we bite
He baas to heaven, plucks our muzzles off,
And bids his chiefest curs be counsellors."

As Barton provided the new words, Hall did the editing, and frequently they clashed. "Hall once objected to a passage of 'pure Barton', and John defended himself, wondering whether he had indeed composed the passage in question. Hall told him not to be silly. To be certain, they looked up the disputed passage: Barton had in fact not written the lines; Shakespeare had."

Though Barton's rewrites were disciplined, he occasionally wrote elaborate passages and Peter Hall kept "a rein on John Barton's literary enthusiasm". Nevertheless, Barton found the heady experience of juxtaposing his words with Shakespeare's hugely enjoyable.

"I enjoyed doing it in such a way that nobody would know where the joints were."

Later in performance this caused consternation, when the critics thought that they had spotted a line with so curious a ring that it must be a fake, but which turned out to be one of Shakespeare's. This led to complaints that the effect of the adaptation was to encourage the exercise of fake-spotting and so prevent their concentration on the plays.

Barton admitted that it gave him a sense of satisfaction to have his work mistaken for Shakespeare's. He was also well able to return the challenge of the purists. At the annual Shakespeare Conference in 1963, Harold Hobson of 'The Sunday Times' approached John Barton and asked him to identify the new scene he had written. Barton replied, "Wait until you have seen the production and then tell me which scene is mine." Hobson failed to pick it out.

Also later, Barton cautioned that where he had been praised for the reworking of early Shakespeare, people had said that "John Barton has written like Shakespeare."

"That is actually strictly untrue, because at that time in his career, Shakespeare was simply writing in an idiom that a lot of Elizabethan playwrights might have used. Shakespeare hadn't, in those early plays, in all the bits that I reworked, come out with an individual authentic voice."

Sheila Bannock, writing in the RSC newspaper in 1976, assessed that "the brilliant textual editing ... was based on a minutely detailed analysis of the vocabulary, imagery and rhythms used by Shakespeare and his contemporaries".

Peter Hall continued to keep John's rewrites to bare narrative, "factual rather than evocative", and, where possible, based verbally on the Chronicles, which were Shakespeare's sources.

"Peter gave me a passage from the Elizabethan chronicler Edward Hall, which he'd taken out of Professor Geoffrey Bullough's 'Narrative and Dramatic Sources in Shakespeare's 'Henry VI'', and I actually cut and edited that particular passage and used it as a prologue for our adaptation."

It became the springboard of the whole production.

"This I say: if you love me you ought to love my child, not for his dessert, but for mine. And since I now shall be taken from you, I charge you all to render your allegiance unto my son, King Henry the Sixth. And as touching the estate of my realm: I command you to love and join together into one league and one unfeigned amity. I will that my brother Humphrey shall be Protector of England during the minority of my child, and that my brother Bedford with the Duke of Burgundy shall rule and be regent of our realm of France; commanding him with fire and sword to persecute Charles, calling himself Dauphin, to the intent either to bring him into obeisance, or to expel him out of our territories.

"What I have gotten, I charge you keep it; I command you defend it; and I desire you to nourish it."

Barton deleted references to Parliament in order to focus on the encounters between the nobles. The texts, written in this way, with added emphasis on their political aspects, "represented a very direct attempt to project an interpretation, not only of Shakespeare but also of history. The directors were, in a sense, writing their own plays alongside Shakespeare's".

Peter Hall explained his belief: "At any given moment, with a given collection of people working together under the chairmanship of their director, there is one way and one way only of expressing the intentions of that play. And those intentions must be expressed in contemporary terms. At any given moment it may mean that there is a slight re-focusing of the dramatist's original intentions.''

So, ''at the risk of historical anachronism'', Barton made Humphrey of Gloucester set up the machinery of ordered government which was ultimately to be used against him because of Henry VI's weakness:

Gloucester: ''Then for the first, let me acquit myself
Of that which Beaufort charges me withal:
Since he avows that I abuse the power
Pertaining to my great protectorship,
How may I better make disproof of this
Than by forgoing a moiety thereof?

Winchester: That should, in sooth, approve your innocence.

Gloucester: Yet I will do it with all willingness,
If you, my lords, approve my purposes:
That is, to achieve some practic of proceeding
To check that canker emulation
Which doth deface our flower of government
For I do fear there's others in this presence
Merit reproach as much as I or Beaufort.

Winchester: Well, sir, your remedy?

Gloucester: Why, thus it is:
When we are met upon some troubled question,
Let us resolve it by our general voice:
And when the matter hath been given vent,
Let the opinion of the greater part
Be straight upheld, and those that are outvoic'd
Yield their intents unto the general.''

One of Barton's most inventive and effective pieces of juxtaposition and creation was an intimate discussion between York and Warwick. Shakespeare had provided a scene between Salisbury, York and Warwick, which ended with Warwick's assertion to York that one day the Earl of Warwick would make the Duke of York a King. From this, John devised a fully developed scene in which he used passages from five different Shakespeare scenes. It became an impressive climax to the first half of their new 'Henry VI'.

Warwick: *''Dost not perceive why these wars were begun?*
*Henry the Fifth, for fear of civil broils,*
*Did lead his peers to France through policy,*
*Dreading lest, lying at home, they should proceed*
*To dangerous question of his doubtful title.*

York: *Beshrew my heart, but I will question it.*
*What,* shall proud Lancaster usurp my right, Part 2 Act 1 Sc 1

*And* hold the sceptre in his childish fist, (242 - 245)
*And* hold the diadem upon his head,
Whose church-like humours fit not for a crown?
*And shall he now surrender up my own?*
*I will not stomach it. What think you, Warwick?*
*May I not claim my own by double title,*
*By right of blood and right of sovereign spirit?*

Warwick; *Why, so thou shalt,* victorious Prince of York, Part 3 Act 1 Sc1
*And till* I see thee seated in that throne (21 - 24)
Which now the House of Lancaster usurps,
I vow by heaven, these eyes shall never close.
*Now, as an earnest of my deep intents.*
*I kneel to thee, professing me thy subject:*
Long live our sovereign Richard, England's King. Part 2 Act 2

York: We thank you, *lord.* But I am not your King Sc 2 (63 - 66)
Till I be crowned and that my sword be stain'd
With heart-blood of the house of Lancaster.

Warwick: *Well, thou* must make fair weather yet a while, Part 2 Act 5 Sc 1
Till Henry be more weak, and *thou* more strong, (30 - 31)
*Only be patient and observe my counsel;*
*And I assure thee* that the Earl of Warwick Part 2 Act 2 Sc 2
Shall one day make the Duke of York a King. (78-79)

York: *I thank thee; let us hence unto my kingdom.*
And, *cousin*, this I do assure myself: (80 - 82)
Richard shall live to make the Earl of Warwick
The greatest man in England but the King."

The second play - the new title being 'Edward IV' - had the best of the original Shakespeare text but, because of the transposition of scenes and telescoping of events in 'Henry VI', it was necessary for John Barton to begin 'Edward IV' with expositional material. As a result, he wrote what amounted to the most concentrated number of new lines in the three plays, leading people to believe that 'Edward IV' contained more new material than 'Henry VI', whereas it actually contained less.

The opening was a declaration by the King expressing his regrets over the past. There were new faces at the Council Board, and the dominance of his wife was evident.

King Henry: "My lords,
Of all the cares that tend upon our crown
That which hath griev'd us most, until this hour,
Hath been that very instrument of order,
Which was devised for our chiefest comfort:
I mean this council board, which should have been

The prop and centre of our government;
But which, by cruel dissent and emulation,
Hath bred a thousand still-lamented sorrows
Within my kingdom and my unquiet soul.
Therefore, my lords, upon the Queen's advice,
We have new-fill'd those places lately voided
By foreign absence and untimely death
With such a kind of gentle councillor,
As only is ambitious for our good.
Therefore we welcome you, good gentlemen,
Lord Say, Lord Clifford, and your valiant son,
And you, Sir Humphrey Stafford: welcome all.

All: Our love and duty to your majesty.

Margaret: Have you no welcome for your princely son?

King: In sooth, I have: most welcome, gentle Edward.
Mark our proceedings well; for in good time
I mean to seat thee in thy father's chair,
(While I myself will lead a private life,
And in devotion spend my latter days.)

Margaret: Yet till that hour devotion must be render'd
Unto your vexed state."

The two lines in parenthesis were original, and it was a marriage of the original with the new which led Frank Cox to the opinion that 'Edward IV' "was the strongest of the three ... a triumph of scholarship and theatrical awareness"; and that "by inspired weeding, contraction, and even in places by brazen invention, he has created from a seldom revived mass of sword-rattling chronicles, a positive addition to the canon of popular works".

The "brazen invention" included a beautifully-constructed scene between King Lewis of France and the Duke of Somerset, in which Lewis refused the tribute due to the English, challenging them as:

"A tedious, churlish and unwelcome guest,
Whom we will lodge, but do not mean to feed,
Whom if you plain, we do not mean to heed,
And whom, when you remove, we will not mourn,
But speed you hence with slight contempt and scorn:
For when thou art in England thy mischance
Is like to prove more fatal than in France."

Originally included towards the end of 'Henry VI', the scene was transferred during rehearsals to become the third scene in 'Edward IV'.

There was little addition to 'Richard III', and what there was appeared as cross-references to the two earlier plays. One piece of emphasis was made, as Barton explained: ''We tried as economically as possible to stress and clarify the importance of the young Princess Elizabeth. (Shakespeare left her out of his play.) To present her and explain her function seemed essential if we were to bring out the historical and thematic point that her marriage with Richmond defined the reconciliation of York and Lancaster, and brought 'The Wars of the Roses' to an end.''

It was also because both Hall and Barton ''were eager to except Richmond from the discredit attached generally to politicians''. Thus, thinks Jonathan Dollimore, the arrival (in Elizabethan terms) ''at the status quo is made to seem received even more satisfying than the (original) text - the one miraculous exception to the otherwise universal human bestiality''.

''The enormously clever elision of three plays into two, with the addition of 'Richard III''' was complete. The chain-smoking, overwork and nights without sleep were over. More than 12,350 lines had been reduced to some 7,450, of which a little over 6,000 came from the original. 1,444 lines were ''first folio Barton''.

It had finally been a race against time. The 1963 Stratford season had opened, with productions of 'The Tempest' and 'Julius Caesar' receiving savage notices. Now, faced with beginning work on what was very much a new, unknown set of unfamiliar plays, an apprehensive Company assembled in the theatre's rehearsal room. They did not know what the future held for them, nor of the historic journey upon which they were all about to embark, as they waited for their director, Peter Hall.

Peter Hall and John Barton *(Gordon Goode)*

Model of the Set *(Geoffrey Wheeler)*

John Bury *(Gordon Goode)*

Ann Curtis *(Gordon Goode)*

Costume Design : Duke of York

Costume Design : Edward IV

Costume Design : Richard, Duke of Gloucester

Costume Design : Lady Elizabeth Grey

Costume Design : Henry VI

Costume Design : Queen Margaret

Costume Design : Humphrey, Duke of Gloucester

Costume Design : The Earl of Warwick

## CHAPTER THREE

### Thursday April 25, 1963

Peter Hall arrived late that morning. The technical rehearsals for the touring production of 'A Midsummer Night's Dream' had finished late the previous evening. He had planned to leave London at 8:15 am, but his Aston Martin wouldn't start. Unable to hire a car for the two-and-a-half hour journey, he travelled to Stratford by train. For him to be late was unusual, as he demanded punctuality of his casts.

Seated on the raked rehearsal stage in the theatre's Conference Hall (now the Swan Theatre), it was a downcast Company that faced him.

"Everything was on the floor," recalls Jeffrey Dench. They were full of doubt and uncertainty. Hall knew of their feelings, and with typical directness he faced the problem head on.

"As a Company you have the greatest reason for anxiety and worry. There's been an extremely hysterical reaction to the opening plays in the season, and people wonder if 'it's one of those years'."

'The Tempest' had opened disastrously "without magic", and "an unimperial Julius Caesar" inauspiciously.

"But," Hall urged, "the work is right and proper and well intentioned."

That said, Hall directed the Company to the mighty task ahead. Ian Holm remembers that when news of the plan to present a new working of the largely unknown 'Henry VI' plays with 'Richard III' was announced it was received with disbelief. During the next hour, as Peter Hall explained how together they would create the vast panorama of dynastic struggle, spirits lifted, enthusiasm grew, there was excitement. For most of them, the plays were unknown so it was to be a journey of exploration.

"We will be in uncharted territory, but the plays are Shakespearean in every aspect: his view of mankind, his view of history, his view of order and his view of character. This is Shakespeare's and no one else's. But it's all early work, particularly Part One, which has a 'Boy's Own Paper' feeling."

Shakespeare grew as he wrote the cycle, and grew in confidence, but it was apprentice work with patches of splendid writing.

Hall reasoned that he could not support the theory that at any point when Shakespeare was not at his best, "he's slung the script to one of his workmates in the theatre and said, 'Write that up will you,' and if there's one good line we are to imagine that Shakespeare is passing by and says, 'Oh no, not that, that!'."

Peter Hall's approach to the text was therefore not made in the belief that Shakespeare did not know his job, but rather that the three 'Henry VI' plays would not hold up over three evenings. Therefore the decision to put in exposition, to cut and clarify, to fudge and borrow developed. It had meant nine months of very hard work, resulting in a different view of Shakespeare's Histories.

"I am perfectly prepared to accept that our version is wrong, but for me it's perfectly justified."

As a result, Hall confessed, many favourite bits had gone. "What favourite bits?" people wondered, until Ian Holm - cast as Richard Gloucester and later Richard III - called out: "Now is the winter of our discontent?" John Barton cut in to assure him that it had indeed been considered!

Shakespeare presented a progressive, organic growth, and Hall saw a series of themes running through the cycle of the three 'reworked' plays, and a succession of waves as "the tide of evil advanced".

The clash of the new ambitious men: their claim to the throne, with a great deal of talk;

Sorcery and the conjuration of spirits;

Prophesies fulfilled;

The humiliation of an arrogant woman, Eleanor of Gloucester, and her husband's grief;

The cunning overthrow and murder of a great and good man with his fatal flaw;

A violent Queen's relations with a weak husband and an ambitious lover;

The punishment of evil men meted out in various ways by other men doing evil to them, or by divine punishment;

Two kinds of civil strife - "plebeian and noble, each adding to these chaos".

"All these themes," Peter Hall explained, "are interwoven to show the evils of selfish ambition and the inability of good men to prevent the disorder that ambition brings."

Each play was then encapsulated. The first play, 'Henry VI', was about human intrigue in the corridors of power, spare and full of saints. The second play, the created title 'Edward IV', was about blood-letting, violence and butchery, full of ladies and very sensual. The third play, 'Richard III', would be the most worrying experience of all.

Henry VI was a visionary; the passage of the molehill at Towton is the Shakespearean voice speaking - to get out of the hurly-burly, retreating to the Forest of Arden, the Golden Times.

Hall cautioned, "If we make these plays Christian, we will be over-simplifying them. If we take a sort of Brechtian view, we will be over-simplifying them, and if we make Richard III a tragic figure, we will be over-simplifying him."

Clearly the dangers were present and the Company had to avoid the traps. He believed strongly that it was a cycle of plunging down into the totalitarian world of Richard III and coming up again with Richmond at the end, and yet feeling that it was all to do again.

"I don't think that Shakespeare is saying, when Richmond arrives as a real progressive force at the end, that we are all going to live happily ever after. His Elizabethan audience could take that, but I think that Shakespeare is more equivocal than that. At the end of any life, you can only be left with a regenerative principle."

Peter emphasised that the arrival of Richmond must be a popular rising against Richard's world but, if the Company had done its job right, the arrival of Richmond must not make the audience feel that it is going to be happy-ever-after. Rather, there is a hopeful pause before the next tragedy begins. Indeed, he believed that, for anyone who would see all three plays, that conclusion would be unavoidable. It had certainly been so when he and John Barton read and worked on the plays.

"Historically the needs of power didn't change. Henry VIII kept on murdering. Elizabeth went on murdering. They had to in order to survive." Then, drawing on the 1963 parallel: "Now the Tory backbenchers are asking for MacMillan's head. Perhaps less bloody, but the same world."

Contemporary similarities to the characters and the incidents in the plays were evident. "The stuff of these plays is still obviously in our lives today. The politics and the power. What you read in your daily paper. What you see on television. The Presidium, the purges, Suez, de Gaulle, Kennedy, Khruschev. The nature of these things is what we must bring as experiences of these plays. Because, first and last, they are a study of power, the need for power and the abuse of power."

It was imperative, Hall continued, that the plays had to be humanised and invested with very rich and subtle character experience, to discover the human being behind the text and thereby reveal the ruthlessness of power.

"If we achieve the right style of playing, I believe that we can get people to understand this nature of power. But we don't want Shakespeare History Acting, because there is a tendency, when actors are playing Shakespeare barons, just to snarl and stamp and rage and roar." He urged them to understand the absolute sincerity, and truthfulness, and candour and honesty of a politician's mask when he's speaking. "I'm not saying that they are lying all the time, but they are certainly wearing a mask all the time, and charm and candour and straightforwardness are parts of the rôles that a politician has to play."

A light, witty speaking of the verse, observing the rhythm and yet not singing it but going for the meaning, was something that Peter Hall had worked at from the very moment he went to Stratford in 1960. It was a flexible, light, tripping delivery of the verse, unsentimental and unsung. It appealed more to the head than to the heart, but made people think what it meant, so in that sense it was highly political.

Indicating three huge stacks of bound, typed texts - red for 'Henry VI', beige for 'Edward IV' and black for 'Richard III' - Hall explained that the "adapted version" had been completed at 9:30 the previous morning, and with ninety-six speaking parts there would be opportunities for everyone. He was aware of the anxiety within the Company about auditions and casting, and that rumours were circulating at the Aldwych Theatre (the Company's London base) of parts in the cycle being raffled! He and Barton would take their time, see everyone, so that there would be full involvement.

He warned, "You will be very, very hard worked, but I'll make it as interesting as possible." He promised boldness and creativity then, with a characteristic flourish, encouraged them "to be a band of arrogant and united heroes".

John Bury's model of the set, made in metal with grilles, walls and throne, sat in front of the Company, who applauded its beauty. In fact, they had never seen anything like it before, and it invoked a world where those passions and instincts which Peter Hall had described could live and breathe.

Bury had made a world of steel. The original concept had been Peter Hall's. His first idea was the image of the sword - cold, keen, death-dealing, cutting edges, force, hardness, strength, embattled. Out of that came the steel mesh metal floor, and out of that came the sound of swords on a metal floor.

"So we started with a texture," recalls Peter Hall, "a style of speaking, a style of presentation, a style of looking, which was all one. It was organic."

The question of costumes was raised by Dame Peggy Ashcroft. She was cast as Margaret, Henry VI's bride, Queen, and widow in all three plays in the cycle. As they were to be presented in one day on several occasions, she was concerned that the costumes would not be heavy. Peter's reply, later forgotten but ironic in view of the subsequent heavyweight robes, dresses, tunics, belts and swords, was an assurance that they would certainly not be.

Peter Hall finished the morning by reading several paragraphs by the Polish writer Jan Kott, whose book 'Shakespeare Our Contemporary' had been given to him in its proof form. He had read it during the train journey that morning, and it became a great influence on the production, copies of the book circulating amongst the actors during rehearsals. The passage on the tragedy of the mole is remembered by everyone present, and had a particular relevance during the weeks of long, exhaustive and exhausting rehearsals which followed.

"There are two fundamental types of historical tragedy. The first, based on the conviction that history has a meaning, fulfils its objective tasks and leads in a definite direction. Tragedy here consists of the cost of history, the price of progress that humanity must pay. The tragic figure then is the man out of step. He who hinders or hurries the relentless steamroller of history must also be crushed by it, simply because he comes too soon or too late ... Man's situation (can be compared) to a mole who unceasingly digs in the earth. A mole lacks awareness, but digs in a definite direction. He has his dreams, but all they do is express dimly his feelings for the sun and the sky. The mole will only be tragic if he happens to be buried by the earth before he reaches the surface.

''There is another kind of historical tragedy, originating in the conviction that history has no meaning but stands still, or constantly repeats its cruel cycle; that it is an elemental force, like hail, storm, hurricane, birth and death ... in this case the mole digs in the earth but will never come to the surface. New generations of moles are being born all the time; they scatter the earth in all directions but are themselves constantly buried by it.

''For a long time he has fancied himself the lord of creation ... that there was a mole's God, who had made moles and promised them a mole-like immortality. But suddenly the mole has realised that he is just a mole; that the earth, sky and stars weren't created for him. He suffers, feels and thinks; but his sufferings, feelings and thoughts cannot alter his fate. He will go on digging in the earth and the earth will go on burying him. It is at this point that he realises he is a tragic mole.''

''That's all right,'' observed Tom Fleming to Jeffery Dench, ''if the mole thinks like a human being!''

HENRY VI: Donald Layne-Smith (Reignier), Peter Geddis (Alencon) Charles Kay (Charles the Dauphin) Janet Suzman (Joan la Pucelle) *(Gordon Goode)*

HENRY VI: The Council Board (1963) Peggy Ashcroft (Margaret)
Michael Craig (Suffolk), John Hussey (Somerset)
John Welsh (Humphrey Duke of Gloucester), David Warner (Henry VI),
Nicholas Selby (Winchester), Clifford Rose (Exeter)
Donald Sinden (York) *(National Geographic)*

HENRY VI: The Council Board (1964) William Squire (Suffolk<br>Philip Brack (Somerset), Peggy Ashcroft (Margaret)<br>David Warner (Henry VI), Nicholas Selby (Winchester)<br>Donald Burton (Exeter), Donald Sinden (York)<br>Brewster Mason (Warwick) *(Stratford Herald)*

HENRY VI: Coronation of Henry VI (1964) Clive Morton (Talbot), David Warner (Henry VI) *(Gordon Goode)*

HENRY VI: John Normington (Bedford), Hugh Sullivan (Burgundy)
Clive Morton (Talbot), David Waller (Williams) *(Gordon Goode)*

HENRY VI: Nicholas Selby (Winchester) *(Stratford Herald)*

HENRY VI: Brewster Mason (Warwick), Donald Sinden (York) *(Gordon Goode)*

HENRY VI: David Warner (Henry VI), Peggy Ashcroft (Margaret) *(Stratford Herald)*

HENRY VI: Capture of Joan. Janet Suzman (Joan) Donald Sinden (York) Brewster Mason (Warwick) *(Geoffrey Wheeler)*

HENRY VI: Peggy Ashcroft (Margaret) Michael Craig (Suffolk) *(Geoffrey Wheeler)*

John Barton re-writing during rehearsals *(Gordon Goode)*

Peggy Ashcroft in her dressing room *(National Geographic)*

Roy Dotrice and David Warner during a break in rehearsals outside The Dirty Duck *(The Dirty Duck)*

## CHAPTER FOUR

The Conference Hall was the shell of the old Memorial Theatre, burned down in 1926, which had been retained when the new Theatre, designed by Elizabeth Scott, was rebuilt and opened in 1932.

Used for rehearsals, the actors liked it and the acoustics were splendid. Entering from the stage door area, there was a large, raked rehearsal stage on the left. On the far right, two curved staircases led to an open balcony. Between was a broad area covered with canvas, on which chairs and benches were grouped. Here the actors sat that morning, each clutching red, beige and black folders.

Janet Suzman - cast as Joan la Pucelle in 'Henry VI' and Lady Anne in 'Richard III' - remembers clearly: "I awesomely looked around and there was somebody called Dame Peggy Ashcroft putting on her glasses, and there was somebody else called Donald Sinden, and there was a young fellow called David Warner, and there were a lot of people who seemed far out of my ken."

Dame Peggy had been the first casting, agreeing to play Margaret before work on the adaptation had even begun. Like many of the leading parts, Donald Sinden had been cast as York after auditioning in John Barton's study in New Cavendish Street during the first months of 1963. John Corvin, a member of the Company for two years and cast as Old Clifford, remembers Sinden, dressed "in a beautiful hand-made suit, shaking hands with everyone, but given a cold shoulder. We were classical actors, and he was the 'Doctor in the House'. How he could play York!"

And to play Henry VI was a young and unknown David Warner, "riddled with insecurity, and nervously looking round at all the actors I had seen when I was at school".

Michael Craig had interrupted a lucrative film career to play the Duke of Suffolk. Long-time Company members were presented with challenging casting: Roy Dotrice as the Duke of Bedford and Edward IV, Ian Holm as Richard III, Clifford Rose as the Duke of Exeter. Newcomers to the Royal Shakespeare Company included Brewster Mason as the Earl of Warwick, Susan Engel as Queen Elizabeth, Nicholas Selby as Winchester, Cherry Morris as the Duchess of Gloucester, John Welch as Humphrey of Gloucester and Charles Kay as George Duke of Clarence.

They all remember the first reading of the text. For Janet Suzman it was "so out of the ordinary, it was such an occasion. When that enormous amount of people were gathered together with roughly put-together scripts. They weren't Arden editions, they weren't Penguins. They were actually scripts which had been cobbled together ... by John Barton and Shakespeare."

"The territory was largely unknown," recalls Nicholas Selby, "the verse was early, and a bit rooty-toot. But the whole thing was *big*, it affected you."

Janet Suzman agrees: "We were all sitting in this room and we were about to embark upon this huge voyage, and I did feel something very special was about to happen, and there was a feeling of 'specialness' about it."

Similar memories are shared by Susan Engel, Cherry Morris, Peter Geddis and Jeffery Dench, who recall "a sense that we were into something monumental and marvellous".

"The readings were gripping," was Brewster Mason's memory, "the plays blazed off the page."

For Donald Sinden, "that reading was one of the most exciting things I have experienced," and he wondered whether it was "a dispirited Company determined to retrieve the wreckage of the season" or the "result of Hall's spirited lecture".

"We read through all three plays over two days, and discovered them as a Company," recalls John Corvin. Ian Holm, not in 'Henry VI', arrived whilst Nicholas Selby was reading. "Quietly, Ian was about to take his seat, when Peter Hall asked him to read the Lord Mayor of London. Ian had not opened his script yet, so glancing over John Hussey's shoulder - who was playing Somerset - he gave a clear reading of the Mayor. Then waited two more hours until it was time for 'Edward IV'."

Roy Dotrice remembers that spirit. "Peter Hall had developed a relaxed and creative atmosphere. The three year contracts meant that the actors were together, their wives mixed, their children mixed and they criticised each others' work. Such a happy time. It was like being back at school with such wonderful mates. But we worked bloody hard!"

"Certainly such a production would not have been possible without a solidly founded Company," is Dame Peggy Ashcroft's belief.

Nicholas Selby maintained a diary of each day's rehearsal calls. It shows the growing intensity of work over the eleven weeks before the first two plays in the Trilogy opened in July.

Rehearsals began at 10 am on Thursday, May 2. From that first day, their bold and open approach to the text and their sustaining of the plot line went to work. Barton's Scene Three, the clash between the followers of Humphrey of Gloucester and the Bishop of Winchester, was vigorously rehearsed and then cut. It was the first of many re-workings of the adapted text. Sometimes because of time, sometimes because it held up the fast movement of the story and sometimes because it lessened their particular political vision.

Then, suddenly, a crisis. Peter Hall collapsed. The years of strain and extreme overwork, the problems and uncertainties - both personal and professional - took their toll. "Nature," it was said, "had presented him with an expensive bill for three and a half years of overwork and worry," and his doctors ordered a complete rest for six months. Hall had yet to acquire what was later to become his highly developed sense to withdraw, and "went down with deep depression and a loss of faith in my talents."

So now John Barton, who was not intended to be among the directors at the outset, was alone to carry forward the immense project. With a young assistant director, Frank Evans, Barton was asked by the actors - Roy Dotrice was their spokesman - to fill Hall's rôle.

An immense asset was Dame Peggy, who nurtured a sense of company spirit and her presence acted as a link between the actors and directorial team.

The first two plays in the Trilogy were rehearsed together as one play, and the 54 scenes were divided between Barton and Evans. Each would rehearse scenes, either in the conference hall or in the dress circle bar, and then swap over for further discussion and work. Six days a week and very often between and after normal performances.

This regimin continued throughout May whilst Peter Hall lay sedated in a darkened room at Avoncliffe in Tiddington.

Then, on Monday, May 27, Hall reappeared at the Theatre. "His eyes dull and sitting uneasily in his chair, running a hand through his hair and looking as if even that effort was too much", he oversaw eight hours of rehearsals. He recalled, "I didn't want to walk into that theatre, I didn't want to see those plays. But I found that if there's a totally self-absorbing job you can do, you can go on doing it however you're feeling". Propped up with cushions in a chair at the top of the staircase in the conference hall, and wearing dark glasses, he watched "the first stagger through" of 'Henry VI' and, two days later, 'Edward IV'.

Ill though he clearly was, Hall was able to see the whole, and know what was needed to lick it into a cohesive shape. He held a Company meeting, giving extensive and detailed notes. Some parts and several scenes were cut. Now rehearsals were intensified and a complicated schedule prepared.

Donald Sinden explains: "The two plays were each divided into some thirty blocks. Each block involved a given number of actors and could be rehearsed without keeping other actors hanging about waiting for their entrances. Each block initially was discussed and the basic moves set by Peter Hall. That group would next move on to the conference hall where John Barton was waiting, and there the same block was repeated, this time with the emphasis on verse speaking and the understanding of the text. The group then moved on to the dress circle bar where with Frank Evans they could again go through the same block, reminding themselves of ideas and moves. Finally, back to the stage for Peter to discuss and set the next block."

Clifford Williams, a fellow director with the Royal Shakespeare Company, explained this process of dual directors. "John had been very instrumental in formulating the concepts and ideas, but acted very often as a - how can I put it? - a 'contrary spirit'. John scrutinised the 'undertext' of the plays to explore all their shades of meaning and cajole his directing partners into seeing the myriad possibilities. Peter Hall then gave Barton's subtexts 'breath', with simple explanations to the actors couched in modern phrases, urging them to find the truth in their *own* reactions."

Cast as Henry VI was a young, inexperienced and rather shy actor; "Dear David Warner," recalls Jeffery Dench, "nine-foot-six and looking like a little boy."

He had been playing the small part of Jim in 'Afore Night Come' by David Rudkin during the RSC's experimental season at the Arts Theatre in London during 1962. The director of that production, Clifford Williams, told Peter Hall about Warner, whose agent subsequently told him that the RSC wanted him to audition for Henry VI.

"I didn't believe him," David remembers. "I knew that he meant that I was to be *in* 'Henry VI', or do some understudy work on 'Henry VI'. 'It's the name part,' he insisted. But I didn't believe him."

Warner auditioned three times. The second was in front of Peter Brook, who noted the "non-actor-actor", picked him as Trinculo for his production of 'The Tempest' and also made a point of telling Peter Hall. Hall auditioned him and was immediately convinced: "David was so right. When he shambled on for his audition, and he did his piece from 'Hamlet', he was just right for Henry ... he had a sweetness."

That evening, Warner was told that he had the part. "But there's a snag, my agent told me, you must sign a three year contract! A wonderful thing for a young actor."

During the early rehearsals for the trilogy, Warner spent a lot of time apologising to the other members of the cast for having got the part. "The embarrassing thing," he remembers, "was my contemporaries from RADA were holding spears whilst I was thrust into star status."

One of his contemporaries, John Corvin, believed, "David was the master of portraying misery on the stage. He was an instinctive actor and he had something within him that broke all the rules. He was given that great confidence by Peter Hall, who allowed him to go on his shambling way, and who encouraged him not to alter his technique."

"To begin with, I just concentrated on being guided by Peter and learning the lines. Then, one fiendish day," David recounts, "a bit of me took over. I don't know what it was. It just happened." He says, "One of the attractions of Henry VI was that it was a relatively unknown rôle, and it was a naturalistic experience for me: I could have easily become the character."

John Corvin adds: "He was very much a 'modern', as opposed to a classical actor. Exceptionally tall, but unheroic in build, he had great audience appeal. For all his height, David had a fragile vulnerability that made him very touching as Henry VI."

Warner remembers, "It was a wonderful experience. I was on to a good thing with that rôle. Henry VI was virgin territory, and there was no great tradition or interpretation looming over me. I was so lucky."

"True," agrees John Corvin, "and look what he had around him, all that cream."

David Warner acknowledges the enormous debt he owes to Dame Peggy Ashcroft. "Working with her was the most sensational opportunity for a young actor. She was superb, helpful, kind, considerate, encouraging, and I was spoilt having someone like her for my first big part. If only I could have been to her what she was to me."

Dame Peggy was an inspiration to everyone. Martin Jenkins, initially cast as a soldier, appreciated the opportunity "to study her supreme artistry. She nurtured a sense of Company spirit, and transformed the actors into a team, working towards a common goal. She sensed when fatigue had set in and when we needed some kind of relaxation. Rehearsing with her was constantly revealing, simply because she possessed the knack of making you feel important - your contribution mattered. People were playing in a diversity of styles of acting, and Dame Peggy gradually drew everyone round to create the epic, canvas style."

At the beginning of rehearsals, there had been general agreement that the cast wouldn't look at the original texts. But Dame Peggy had been very concerned about all the cutting and insertions, and would only say the lines in her copy of the Temple edition of 'Henry VI'. Until one morning, "John Barton smuggled in a speech he had written, pretending it was written by Shakespeare, and convinced her to include it." After that, the Temple edition was laid aside. "This is what we're doing," she decided. "Let's have a go at it and let's make it work."

Dame Peggy had "plotted the trajectory of the character (Margaret) which, in the course of the three plays, must age from 27 to 80".

"She began as a scared young girl captured on a battlefield - whose first entrance was strengthened during rehearsals by the addition of the invented off-stage words: 'I'll not go with thee. Knowst thou who I am?' She went on," remembers Robert Potter, "to captivate King Henry, to defend him and dare his enemies to battle. As her armies rolled on, with a wagon that made her a royal Mother Courage, down the path to disaster, she became ever more resolute, transgressing astonishingly from heroism into vindictive cruelty in the climactic 'paper crown' scene, taunting the captured York as she strutted about him. From these dizzying heights she toppled into the horror of Tewkesbury and a tragic, retributive come-uppance, held writhing while her only son was butchered by the sons of York - and on from there to preside, in her old age and prophetically withered beauty, over the rise and fall of Richard III that ended the bloodshed ... and returned us with relief and amazement to the ground, much wiser, in the relative safety of the early 1960s."

Martin Jenkins remembers: "Even today I can still hear many of her speeches inside my head - still catch the inflections, the strength of passion and the sounds of her distinctive rolling French 'r'."

"I had heard Scottish ladies vocalise with a similar sound," suggested Donald Sinden, "it came from the back of the throat as if she were gargling."

Dame Peggy explained: "The essential thing about Margaret was that she was a foreigner. Peter agreed with the French 'r'. When rehearsals were over he said, 'I don't think you need it,' but I couldn't possibly abandon it then."

Peter Hall's view of Margaret was that she embodied the curse on the Houses of York and Lancaster. Dame Peggy's particular attraction to the part was that she had to bring her lover's head on stage.

"That seemed to me a tremendous challenge; something I looked forward to very much. How could you play a scene like that and convince an audience? That 'happening' affected the character, and explained her later bestiality - especially the taunting of York: to wipe blood all over somebody's face. Those are the things that excite you about a part. I mean, they seem so melodramatic that you say to yourself, 'Well, how can you possibly get away with that, make it believable?', and then you want to try. I felt it would be central to the nature of the character."

In performance, it was the final scene of the first play, 'Henry VI', and showed John Barton at his most inventive. He whipped a stirring climax out of bits from seven different Shakespeare scenes from Parts One and Two of 'Henry VI', plus "his own concoctions and the odd lines from 'Gorboduc'. The effect was to throw the final focus on Margaret, entering with the head of her slain lover, Suffolk", (whose murder by a vengeful and baying mob was not announced, as in Shakespeare, but seen. His head was hacked off and then tossed against the double oak doors of the set) "bending her wild grief and anger into a protective embrace of her weak husband, and breathing defiance to their enemies."

Michael Billington has written that the great mystery of her performance lay not in the transition from youth to age, startling though that was, but the venom and passionate hatred she was able to present.

Donald Sinden remembers the scene where Margaret daubs York's face in the blood of his dead child. There suddenly came a point when he saw in the eyes of Dame Peggy - the Hampstead wife and mother - a genuine hatred. "The character had completely taken over. You often see this in an attitude, a face, a voice; with Peggy you saw it in furious close-up. I thought, 'she can't hate me - we've just had a cup of tea together.' At the end of that scene, the entire Company of sixty actors remained in complete silence for quite a minute before continuing with the play."

"It was real, my God!" recalls John Corvin. "A towering performance. That scene just grew and grew and went on growing."

Dame Peggy considers that the seemingly impossible bestial act was credible as a result of the violence that had been perpetrated on her lover. "Shakespeare has drawn a woman of passion - treacherous certainly, but never less than human and believable."

For Sinden too, the scene presented particular emotions. "York goes off to war with his three older sons, Edward, Richard and George, leaving his seven-year old Rutland at home. He becomes separated from his sons in the heat of battle and is captured by the commander of the Lancastrian forces (Margaret). York is taunted about his son. Where's Edward? He doesn't know. Where's Richard? He doesn't know.

Where's George? He doesn't know. But he's not giving anything away. But he knows that he's left Rutland at home, so when Margaret slaps his face with the napkin soaked in his son's blood, I imagined that it was my own son, who happened to be eight-years old at the time."

Margaret: "Where are your mess of sons to back you now?
The wanton Edward, and the lusty George?
And where's that valiant crook-back prodigy,
Dicky your boy, that with his grumbling voice
Was wont to cheer his dad in mutinees?
Or, with the rest, where is your darling Rutland?
Look, York, I stain'd this napkin with the blood
That valiant Clifford, with his rapier's point
Made issue from the bosom of the boy;
And if thine eyes can water from his death,
I give thee this to dry thy cheeks withal."

The scene was pure Shakespeare, although in his three drafts for their new texts, Barton had made cuts and transposed some lines.

In rehearsal, John responded to demands for amendment and rewrites, and the text was continually adjusted.

"He had such a fertile imagination," recalls John Corvin.

"He could come up with ten ideas and Peter would use two," adds Hugh Sullivan. A copy of the Third Draft shows Barton's many textual suggestions and interpretations, and the staging possibilities, followed by Hall's 'Yes' or 'No' reaction. "That was Peter Hall's genius, he could look at the whole vista."

Substantial rewriting was done overnight, but he astonished the actors by being able "to pluck one-liners out of the air".

One occasion was the rehearsal of the fight between York (Donald Sinden) and Old Clifford (John Corvin) in 'Edward IV'. Corvin had the lines:

"Nor should thy prowess want praise and esteem
But that 'tis shown ignobly and in treason"

before the clash of swords. Hall turned to Barton, who was busily writing lines for a different scene: "He can't just stand there, he needs a line to bring him into the fight." John looked up, thought for a minute and said,

"And that I'll prove against thee with my sword."

That fight was one of the highlights of the Trilogy. Heavy, six-foot, two-handed swords were used, which created a marvellous effect.

Barton, who arranged all the fights, told Donald Sinden: "As you come in, scrape your sword along the floor, swing it over your head and bring the downward stroke towards John, who parries the blow with his sword."

Corvin continues the story. "We had doubts. We couldn't lift, and we couldn't parry. As Donald came towards me, really fierce, dragging the sword across the floor, sparks flying, he gave a yell and a heave to bring it down towards my head; I was to heave up my sword, scraping it across the floor - sparks - with a tremendous clang. Fantastic! But I couldn't lift my sword in time, and I saw this massive six-foot sword coming towards me. I just dropped my sword and ran."

In performance, the two heavily armoured lords circled the vast empty stage, whilst the amplified crashes of their enormous swords encapsulated the ferocious dynastic struggle. It was electrifying, brutal and terrifying. The titanic will of York finally drove the exhausted Clifford to the floor.

Barton had developed a technique of making stage flights and battles *look* as dangerous as possible, while at the same time ensuring maximum safety. His belief was that the audience must never feel that the actors are in any physical danger but are in complete control, "safe and theatrical". Peter Hall had been troubled about the nature of the many battles in 'The Wars of the Roses', and in early January had written a note to Barton:

> "The starting point of these productions of the History plays is to create a dangerous world of cold steel. Elegant, yet barbarous; symmetrical, yet harsh. The danger of power politics and the dangerous nature of these men for all their medieval background, and the fact that they select something as decorative as a rose as their symbol, can never be forgotten.
> This danger and violence is expressed constantly through the plays in terms of physical conflict. What therefore to do about the battles?
> I do not believe that the naturalistic battles that we had in 'Troilus' are a solution for what we need. Even if we can bring the actors to the point of doing the battles supremely well, there is still something comical and mock heroic to our age in seeing two men bashing at each other with swords ...
> but whatever the physical and visual image is on the stage, it must be one of danger which affects the modern audience deeply ...
> Would a slow motion, fully acted-out battle do if the swords, shields and battle axes were of monumental weight and size and danger?"

Barton created a panoramic galaxy of sword fights and battles, each different from the one before, and remembered for their great excitement.

Frank Cox wrote, "With a text which requires almost every major character to wield a sword, the pitfalls of the old time 'One-two Oh, I am slain' stage fight are negotiated with deceptive ease; not for one moment is that familiar sense of the ludicrous allowed to tinge the numerous but never bewildering encounters of steel and wood."

The fights had an additional excitement for the audience.

"The front row got everything," says Jeffery Dench. "A sword shot off the stage and fixed itself in a seat between two ladies; a flaming torch rolled onto a lady's lap and was furiously stamped out by her husband, who never took his eyes off the actors on stage, who in turn were fascinated by his acrobatics."

Peter Hall's suggestion of elegance and barbarity in the battles and weaponry of great size and danger was also his concept for the world in which the production would live. It became his directive to the designer, John Bury: "Steel, chased steel, engraved steel, will create a world of danger and of elegance, harshness and formality."

That was enough for John Bury, who visualised an elaboration of sword, shield and plate armour. During his early experiments with shapes and textures, he showed Peter Hall a piece of expanded metal floor. Slowly dragging a sword across the metal, Hall exclaimed: "And *that's* the sound we want."

Bury's method of design was a very radical, unconventional realism. "It's not naturalism I'm after, but the sense of a thing actually being a thing. For instance, I've got to know what sort of noise it's going to make when you hit it. And I can't even start to make a model until I've found the right materials - the texture is the language I'm looking for. I can't start making a model in balsa wood and then say this has got to be made in iron. I don't draw and my painting is rudimentary."

John Bury went to Stratford as a guest designer in 1962, following eighteen years with Joan Littlewood's Theatre Workshop. "In my use of materials at that time, I was resolutely against falsehood. One thing I never did was to pretty things up, not transmute everything into fairytale unreality of canvas and scene paint. I was searching for a theatre in which anything painted on canvas would seem unreal."

He used real materials like bricks, corrugated iron, paving stones and old tarpaulins. Desmond Hall, who was Production Manager at Stratford when Bury arrived, remembers, "John could do a whole show for £5 with bits out of a field."

"At Stratford," Bury says, "I had to reconsider my views on materials. I had to make real textures but, this time, out of artificial materials. Fortunately, the plastics industry was expanding and all sorts of synthetic materials, such as expanded polystyrene and polyurethanes, were coming on the market. This led to an entirely new function for the paint shops, creating surfaces rather than painting them. Surfaces which were the right weight, density and reflective index, in addition to the right colour."

The decision to set 'The Wars of the Roses' in a world of hard steel presented a problem. "Thick steel plate was, of course, too heavy to use. A series of experiments were carried out with thin steel and iron sheeting, and the problems which immediately arose were that, although we needed the glint and luminous surface of metal, we could not accept large flat reflective areas. The hard new surface of a thin steel sheet, seen from a distance, looked no more metallic than a piece of ply-board. We worked on the surface of iron and steel with various corroding agents such as acids."

Desmond Hall recalls that Scenic Artist John Collins used so much acid that it was literally running along the floor of the paint shop. Yet it only achieved a patchy rustiness, which gave a romantic atmosphere rather than the desired feeling of strength.

John Bury continues: "The Theatre had previously used small quantities of copper foil, and on these occasions sulphides had been used with great success in tarnishing the copper." It was this technique which was to solve the problem.

"A trade preparation called 'Sisal-Craft' was used, which consisted of a very thin layer of electronically deposited copper. This was mounted on bitumen paper made for thermal insulation and fixed on plates of hardboard half an inch thick. The sheets were moulded to give the shape required and then treated with sulphide. But, when applied directly to the copper, the ammonium sulphide produced a very patchy effect. It was necessary to wet the copper with a wetting agent - mild detergent - and then keep feeding the surface with stronger and stronger solution of ammonium sulphide."

"John lived in a world of sulphuric acid," Desmond Hall remembers with amusement, "and the smell was terrible."

Bury also went to Bird's scrapyard in the Birmingham Road, and bought a vast amount of thin metal sheets which had almost rotted away - some having a 'lace' effect. Those not rusty enough were treated with acid.

Walking from his workshop at Avonside in Mill Lane in his customary boiler suit and rubber boots, he passed the 'Dirty Duck'. On the balcony was a stage designer to whom Bury's work was anathema. For all to hear he called out: "There goes the bloody cement mixer!"

All the sheets and plates were fixed on two huge walls which dominated either side of the stage. These could be moved into almost any position, "to diminish or increase the shape of the acting area, and for battle scenes (they) could be swung off to allow a completely bare stage." Roy Dotrice adds, "The set made it easy to act on that stage; the walls pushed you towards the audience."

"The main floor of the set had a 1 in 18 rake, and was made out of expanded steel. Great care had to be taken that expanded metal was laid so that the reflective surfaces faced the audience." Bill Lockwood in the prop shop spent hours on the telephone finding the right steel - "It had to have the ring."

In 1962, the prop shop was in what had been Randle Ayrton's little theatre in grounds at Avoncliffe. It had been transferred complete to New Street, next to the Carpenters' Shop. Here Bury experimented with the texture for the steel for the stage floor. It was sometimes very hazardous. The sheets were immersed in a large acid bath which gave off nitrous fumes, so he needed to work out of doors.

"We found that on windy days the effervescent spray would blow onto our faces as we worked. In the end we had to wear goggles and cover any exposed skin with protective cream."

For additional effects, some sheets were dumped for several days into the River Avon.

The steel sheets were finally covered with an overlay of wire mesh of about three quarters of an inch aperture. Clifford Rose calls it "the cheesegrater surface".

"You laid very carefully when you died," remembers Jeffery Dench, whilst John Corvin asserts, "There are 'Wars' actors who still have the diamond impression from so much kneeling."

Towards the end of the season, and in time for the return of the productions in 1964, the armourer Tony Watts produced a stock of special metal knee caps. Brian Davenhill, now Head of the Scenic Workshop, remembers being on his knees throughout the night, as he adjusted the wire mesh to the floor to the dimensions of the Aldwych Theatre stage, when the productions moved there in January 1964.

"I passed through a series of thresholds of pain! I was grateful that I didn't have to repeat the process when the plays returned to Stratford."

Bury had created "a great steel cage of war, a world where the passions could be alive." Mike Leigh, the playwright, who observed the rehearsals, has never forgotten the impact of the set: "What was extraordinary was the sense of things being real."

Pamela Howard, Director of Theatre Design at St. Martin's College of Art and Design in London, recalls: "It was a definite landmark. And it did shock. Nobody expected raw materials in the theatre, it was the end of illusionist theatre."

Ann Curtis, who collaborated with John Bury on the costumes, recalls that the first time she saw the set, "it looked like two great tanks. The use of metal summed up the plays; it was power that was being fought for - and connived for. It was a saga."

Two props dominated the set: the thirteen foot long pentagonal council table and the oversized throne that was run on and off stage by tracks, "often empty, but prominent as a recurring symbol of the popularity of power".

"John was a massive man - 'the Great Bear' we called him - and everything he put on that set was massive. The chairs and benches were massive, the torches and swords were massive, and we had huge 'Mother Courage' carts," recalls Peter Geddis. And Ted Valentine, who joined the production in 1964, adds: "He designed to his own size."

Cherry Morris remembers, "Those huge, thundering walls moving into place and nearly running down any actors not on the ball. Philip Brack (as the Duke of Burgundy) was one who was squashed into his armour. We used to say that in most productions actors have to make the props look heavy, but with John's set the problem was to make the props look as though they were light enough to lift."

Bury's belief was that there should be a prop which became an 'image object' for every situation.

So many swords were needed that it required the work of several blacksmiths at Archer's Foundry on the Birmingham Road, and for weeks Bob Tustain, Archie Hopkins and others hammered out the mild steel - which also had to possess the special 'ring' both Hall and Bury wanted.

One additional definition of the stage picture was the carefully directed lighting, which was primarily white.

"This was a point of principle," John Bury affirms. "Real materials need real light."

John Russell Brown has written that, "By using real-looking surfaces, especially simulated steel-sheet on the stage floor, the light was variously reflected or absorbed, and so a general indication of atmosphere was achieved.

"The costumes reflected the metal world, and were revolutionary. We said to ourselves, 'If the world is steel, the people are the jewels in this metallic setting.' I wanted to take the fancy dress out of costumes, and Peter emphasised that they must be neither literally historical nor literally unhistorical."

"Peter Hall said, 'Too rigid adherence to historical accuracy tends to create stuffed dummies,'" remembers Ann Curtis. "Costumes should be clothes, not costumes; worn enough to suggest the necessary period connotations; contemporary enough to free bodies of the actors and the minds of the audience."

Ann Curtis had been a ladies' cutter in the Wardrobe Department for three years, and a portfolio of her designs had been sent to Peter Hall. It was John Wykham, the Technical Administrator, who asked Ann to help John Bury with the costumes for the Histories. (Later in the programme, to her delight, the "help" became "collaboration".) Working from a small office next to the Conference Hall, she had a deadline of eight weeks to produce designs for hundreds of costumes, which she remembers as "an exhausting but joyous experience." Her method was to create a silhouette of the period and build freely around it.

"The costumes were not all academically-historically accurate in every detail. I worked for an overall historical shape with lots of modern materials and textures. Everyone was broad-shouldered, which was a period detail we pushed further. We made our own rules."

John Bury explained his design concept: "The costumes corroded with the years. The once-proud red rose of Lancaster became as a rusty scale on the soldiers' coats; the milk-white rose of York was no more than a pale blush on the tarnished steel of the Yorkist insurrection. Colour drained and drained from the stage until, among the drying patches of scarlet blood, the black night of England settled on the leather costumes of Richard's thugs."

The materials for the costumes were unbleached calico, floor-cloth (a mixture of twill-weave cotton and jute) and leatherised suede cloth. All were made under the supervision of Emma Selby Walker in the Wardrobe Department. They were then taken next door to the Paint Shop where John Bury had organised groups of local people and students from the Slade School to apply the texture.

This was the "gunking process" when thick liquid latex - looking like heavy milk - was coated onto the costumes. The idea was then to apply various colouring agents, but these were found to produce a chemical inpatability and the costumes soon fell to pieces.

After playing around with different methods, the successful solution was to ''gunk'' the costumes and, whilst still wet, throw on a mixture of glue crystals, marble chippings, chicken grit and stone gravel which someone had swept up from the tennis courts in Southern Lane.

Bury says, ''We shook the costumes, the excess grit fell out, and the impression left was an interesting design.''

''At first Peter Hall thought that they looked like rags,'' recalls Ann Curtis, ''but on stage with lights he was delighted with the lustrous effect. It was a great moment.''

''Once the costume shape was right,'' says Joe Clark, who was the principal men's cutter, ''there were no seaming problems because of the gunking. But we couldn't alter a costume because although the 'gunk' was pliable at first, it later went stiff like old rubber tyres.''

It also made the costumes very heavy. ''There was a Palace revolt,'' says Bury. ''The actors told me that they could never work in them, but they grew used to them. So much, in fact, that for fun they occasionally did a tap-dance routine in the Green Room.''

Hall told them, ''You look marvellous. At present the costumes are wearing you, but you will grow into them.''

Brewster Mason took his costume home and weighed it, whilst Donald Sinden was discovered in his dressing room wearing only shorts, and weighing first his belt and then his costume. ''And reporting back to us,'' says Clifford Rose, ''with a mixture of astonishment and pride that it was 56 lbs.''

It was Sinden, who following a morning rehearsal in his costume on the stage, appeared at the Wardrobe Department asking for 'the Gunk Department', and left a road sign outside reading 'Loose Chippings'.

Certainly the heaviest costume was David Warner's long Coronation robe for Henry VI. Made of the floor-cloth material, it was decorated with large pieces of brass strip castings, which wore away the stitching at every performance. Susan Engels' costume as Queen Elizabeth allowed little freedom of movement. The weight of Nicholas Selby's gave him 'the Winchester Walk', and Cherry Morris' (as the Duchess of Gloucester) ''on that raked stage almost carried me straight out to the audience.''

''My costume was already quite heavy,'' says Clifford Rose, ''before the 'gunking' process was set in motion - after, it seemed like several hundredweight more. Then it went through a further process known as 'breaking it down' when yet more paint was added. Then a belt went on like a diver's - lead weights all round. And finally, for a number of scenes, armour was worn over all this as well. The culmination was reached in the Coronation scene for 'Henry VI', when a suitably elaborate, and of course, heavy, Coronation robe was thrown over all that had gone before.''

Temporarily delighted was Tom Fleming. His costume arrived 'ungunked'.

"He was so pleased," says Jeffery Dench, "and he locked it away in the wardrobe in his dressing room. Next day it was still locked away in the wardrobe, but it had been 'gunked'!"

Boots were 'gunked' in rows of thirty at a time in the Territorial Army Hall in Broad Street. The liquid sometimes dropped inside, and Ann Curtis saw Jeffery Dench hurl a boot - the toe had stuck solid - out of the window of his dressing room. "And our decision on long leather boots for the principals caught a creative moment," she says, "when that autumn they appeared in fashion houses like Courèges and in 'Vogue' magazine.

"There was also an outcry about the weight of the broad iron and lead belts, which were hung on the costumes by industrial pelixan hooks. So, unknown to John Bury, Tony Watts produced a set in rubber, but the actors wanted the heavy ones back, because 'it helped the balance'."

Metal armour came from a stock which had been used in the time of Sir Barry Jackson's directorship in the 1940s.

"We polished it and tarted it up," recalls Tony Watts. "John didn't want the 'Camelot' look. But after each performance it needed repair. I kept a box by the Green Room - 'Armour in here' - and it was never empty!"

The chain mail was made by knitting thick butcher's string into five-foot length strips, covered with silver lacquer and then beaten flat. Afterwards a fibreglass compound was painted on to obtain the 'fall' or 'shine'. All the ladies in the Company, secretaries and friends were allocated their ball of string and two thick needles.

"It was like knitting for Victory," remembers Dame Peggy.

Most of the costumes have either disappeared or disintegrated, but a small number have survived. Their size, weight and texture reflect both the stamina of the actor and the stature of the character he portrayed. They are the tangible memories of this famous production and of the sensational new direction that was taken in costume design.

At the beginning of June, the Theatre announced a postponement of the opening dates for the first two productions in 'The Wars of the Roses'. Peter Hall's absence from rehearsals had made it impossible to complete the work in time, and the first performances would be put back two weeks.

The maelstrom of activity intensified. The rehearsal call sheet for Monday, June 17 represents the growing pressure:

<u>Conference Hall</u>

| | |
|---|---|
| 10:00 | Notes (Henry Act 2) |
| 11:00 | Scene 27 (7th Council)<br>All name parts |
| 12:00 | Scene 29 (8th Council) |

<u>Circle Foyer</u>

| | |
|---|---|
| 12:00 | Scene 46 to 50<br>Scene 51 and 54<br>All speaking parts |

| | | |
|---|---|---|
| | All name parts | |
| 1:00 | Scene 31 (Kenilworth Scene) | |
| | All name parts | |
| 2:00 | Scene 32 (Dartford Scene) | 2:00 Mr. Smith |
| | All concerned | 2:30 Mr. Wynne |
| 3:00 | Scene 40 (1st Tower Scene) | 3:00 Mr. Corvin |
| | Mr. Holm, Mr. Normington, | 3:30 Scene 44 (10th Council) |
| | Mr. Marsden, Mr. Jenkins, | All name parts |
| | Mr. Knowles, Mr. McConnochie | 4:30 Scene 33 (Iden Scene) |
| 3:30 | Scene 41 (2nd Tower Scene) | All concerned |
| | Mr. Warner, Mr Selby, | |
| | Mr. Geddis, Mr. Jennings, | plus rehearsals of the |
| | and Master. Menzies | armies of York and Warwick |
| 4:15 | Scene 41 (2nd Tower Scene) | |
| | and Scene 42 (3rd Tower Scene) | |
| | All concerned except | |
| | Mr. Dotrice, Mr. Holm, | |
| | Mr. Kay and Mr. Brack. | |
| 5:30 | Mr. Sinden | |
| 7:00 | Mr. Welch | |
| 8:00 | Miss Suzman | |
| 9:00 | Mr. Geddis | |
| 9:30 | Mr. Selby | |

''Peter Hall created a marvellous working atmosphere,'' recalls John Corvin. ''He never raised his voice and he never lost his sense of humour. We weren't fooled by the charm and the lovely smile and the boyishness. He had very watchful eyes which would narrow if something displeased him. You *had* to be sincere, and he came down like a ton of hot bricks with any sign of sentimentality in a performance. He hated sentimentality and the operatic style of acting. You *had* to be sincere.''

''Most of the time he sat quietly,'' remembers Roy Dotrice, ''hunched at the edge of the stage puffing his pipe. He worked by the merest suggestion, allowing the actors to *think* that they were doing something they had worked out for themselves. There was little tension and no tantrums. He had such charisma.''

Charles Kay agrees: ''His approach was so sure and his vision of how it was to be so clear, that the whole cast, experienced and inexperienced alike, absorbed it joyfully and moved as one to bring it about.''

''Being young and unafraid,'' says Ian Holm, ''we plunged headlong into the work.''

''I received all the plusses from Peter Hall,'' recalls David Warner, ''warmth and encouragement. I was very much an instinctive actor, and he gave me a free rein.''

''As rehearsals went on, it became clear that this was going to be a very contemporary, tough, unsentimental production. I remember thinking, are there to be no warm or sympathetic presentations of characters in this cycle?'' remembers Clifford Rose. ''All seemed to be twisted to show corrupt or self-seeking motives. Nobility was out!''

For Robert Potter, a Fulbright scholar writing a dissertation on medieval drama, ''The struggle for power and domination was unrelenting and unforgiving, like a sequence of vendettas in a gangster epic, and very much as bloody. If we were in the Middle Ages at all, it was definitely not in the 'Très Riches Heures' of the Duc de Berry, but lost in the fog, mud and sweat of some forgotten mediaeval battlefield. And, although it was also like a film, the film definitely wasn't 'Ivanhoe' - more like Ingmar Bergman's 'The Seventh Seal'.''

John Barton was always absorbed in the rehearsals, and this led to what Donald Sinden calls ''Bartonisms''.

''He would stand with a razor blade and 'sharpen his finger','' claims Roy Dotrice. ''John *was* Epihodov from 'The Cherry Orchard'.''

John Corvin remembers, ''He would crash through swing doors, slither down six stairs in one go. On one occasion whilst giving notes in the Green Room, John sat on the counter. Then he got down to give a direction to an actor before jumping back onto the counter. But Gladys - who ran the Green Room - had lifted the flap and John disappeared.''

Ian Holm interrupted a passionate dissertation to point out that the leg of the chair on which Barton was rocking, had been diving in and out of his coffee cup for some minutes, holding his audience too spellbound to pay any attention to his views. Donald Sinden remembers that John was always giving notes and no actor could escape.

''He discovered that several of the Company popped across to the 'Dirty Duck' during their one-hour-exactly lunch break from rehearsals. He took to wandering around the bar. Hoping to distract him, actors would invite him to have a drink - but to no avail. He accepted and continued his tracking, glass in hand.''

In rehearsals, he drove himself. Always chain-smoking, hunched and gesturing with his elbows, continually referring back to the very process of interpretation itself - the 'unlocking' (one of Barton's favourite words in rehearsal) of the sense and emotion contained in Shakespeare's structures. He concentrated on keeping a strong narrative line through the scenes, telling the actors sympathetically: ''I know you're tired, so take it very easily now. Please fight gently. It's the positions and timing we want.'' And despite the tiredness - rehearsals, in addition to the normal mornings and afternoons, were now held after the close of an evening's performance, and did not finish until 5 am, six days a week - a disciplined silence was observed.

Time was the enemy and sleep was short. Ann Curtis remembers that she and John Bury never seemed to sleep. ''Once rehearsals were over, Peter gave notes for an hour and then John Barton would give line interpretation. Then at 5 am the technical notes were covered. Between 6 am and 7 am, John and I would correlate our notes before dashing to the carpenters, the wardrobe, John Collins and the Prop Shop for the work to be ready in time for when rehearsals recommenced at 10 am. John would often fall asleep in his chair in the Conference Hall, which led to John Barton declaring that, 'John Bury never watches anything, he's always asleep!'''

Throughout the final week of June, rehearsals continued all day and night, even during performances of 'Julius Caesar', 'The Tempest' and 'The Comedy of Errors'.

Roy Dotrice explains: ''John Barton had *great* enthusiasm. He would wait in the wings and catch people as they came off stage, and get them into the Conference Hall to rehearse a scene. Sometimes with only minutes between entrances, and even when a quick change was involved.''

''I remember that!'' says Jeffery Dench. ''And the stage manager counted off the seconds before we had to rush back to the stage, still with John beside us, giving notes!''

The dress rehearsal for 'Henry VI' began at 12:30 in the morning and ended at 4:30 a.m. on Monday July 1, and this followed a full rehearsal on the Sunday.

''I remember coming out of the stage door with Dame Peggy at a quarter past nine in the morning,'' Peter Hall recalls, ''and we had started at two the previous Sunday afternoon. It was madness, but it did give you the opportunity to put things together at white hot intensity.''

''One thing about that dress rehearsal stands out for me,'' recalls Nicholas Selby. ''It was in the middle of the night after a very long day, and we all stood in the respective wings, chatting, fiddling with our unknown costumes. And then, as we processed to the crowning of Henry VI, we heard for the first time, Guy Woolfenden's music. It was a shattering moment. Tiredness and unease fell away, and the music seemed to draw together all the work and effort of the whole Company up to that point.''

Originally, the music for the production was to have been composed by Raymond Leppard, the Company's music adviser, but his other commitments took him away from Stratford. So Peter Hall asked the young Guy Woolfenden, who had joined the RSC that year as an assistant music director. Hall's directive to him was to seek out an interpretation of the dangerous world of the Cycle.

''The music has to have historical connections, but not be literal. It also can't be 'modern'. To have conventional trumpets, horns and drums is going to sound like Kneller Hall, and keeps us in a world of pomp and circumstance and 'Long Live the Empire'. The fanfares should be dangerous - short, sharp and of a 'strange' noise. I think the drums should be very slack so that their tone is low and ominous.''

''I tried to match John Bury's 'World of Metal' set'', Guy Woolfenden has explained, ''with a harsh metallic noise, using a brass ensemble with percussion.''

Seven musicians produced all the music - Gordon Bennett, Gilbert Cobbett, David James, James Kirby, Derek Oldfield, Gareth Richards and James Walker - and much of it was played by them on stage and in costume, sometimes as soldiers of York and sometimes of Lancaster.

"The music cues had to be memorised, with the moves, word cues, costume changes, and no conducting possible to ensure ensemble. To facilitate this, I wrote the music into small note books, which the players could check before going on stage. These were then secreted in the regulation thigh-boots, though I daresay a few were consulted behind a convenient shield or dead body."

Several sounds were obtained from instruments specially made for the production. One was a great curving bronze horn with a tone somewhere between a trumpet and a French horn. Played in duet with a long coach horn, they produced stirring abstract effects. Another, invented by Woolfenden and Leppard, was an oblong box about seven foot high and fitted with tautened piano strings. The edge of a dagger was carefully drawn down the strings, which created a weird, wild, unnerving hum.

Peter Geddis remembers one problem. "All the recordings of explosions and cannon sounded either like pop-guns or dustbins clanging together. So Guy hit upon a brilliant idea.

"I persuaded eight or ten people - including Peter Hall - to blow up empty crisp packets and burst them in quick succession," Guy recalls, "and these were then recorded, played back at half-speed and the gaps edited out."

For two more weeks the pace of rehearsal was maintained, ending with a weekend of four dress rehearsals. Both productions were to open on Tuesday, July 17, with 'Henry VI' in the afternoon and 'Edward IV' in the evening. "The whole company had worked extremely hard for many weeks; too hard actually," Donald Sinden has said. "We were dropping and we had no reserves of energy, with the result that the final dress rehearsal was a fiasco, and the company was dispirited as we gathered on the stage for notes from Peter and John. The production that we hoped would salvage the reputation of the Company seemed a failure to us all, and in approximately twenty hours the public and the press would witness another disaster."

Hall complimented them on their work and told them that what they were now doing was absolutely perfect.

Brewster Mason recalled: "He had such dynamism, such conviction of purpose. He knew the feeling of the company, and precisely what had to be said. He was a superb tactician and politician."

Donald Sinden agreed: "It was like Henry the Fifth rallying his troops."

For Peter Hall, the whole experience had not been a happy one. "I remember it as fairly awesome and hideous actually. The size of the undertaking, and the pressure I had on me - both personal and professional - made it a very difficult time. So I don't look back on it as a golden moment at all. It was a bit like an endurance test. I enjoyed it once it was over, because I could see that we had put something on the stage which was particular, and was speaking to the audience at that moment in very clear terms."

The long months of rehearsal had brought little diminution to the great pressure on Peter Hall, and both he and John Barton had almost worked themselves into the ground. There was still 'Richard III' to come, but they had created a fine Company and nurtured a strong spirit. By 10 pm on Tuesday, July 17, they knew that all their effort had been triumphantly worthwhile.

At the end of 'Edward IV', the audience rose to acclaim their unique achievement, and the critics were unanimous in their praise. R.B. Marriott in 'The Stage' acknowledged this fact: "If there has been a discordant note among the critics, I have not come across it. In fact, rarely has a venture in the theatre received such praise and support."

The Coventry Evening Telegraph called it "A gruelling, demanding and wonderful experience ... The impact was tremendous, so that we left Stratford last night mentally exhausted, our senses stirred by a whole range of emotion," whilst The Birmingham Mail asserted: "Let me say at once that Peter Hall's production, in magnificently sombre and serviceable sets by John Bury, is quite splendid ... This is a collector's piece."

R.B. Marriott's article recognised the production as a Company achievement. "With this memorable production we see just what the Company can do, and are given a vision of what we may fairly expect them to do in the future. Of course, we might in any case have had a splendid production of these plays, finely acted and of striking interest. But qualities of an ensemble of players, of a Company that has been working together with a purpose and with a long term policy, are apparent as never before in a modern British Shakespeare production."

"This is a young Company, not depending on stars. It happens that Peggy Ashcroft is playing Queen Margaret, but like the serious, unshowy artist that she is, she works for and with the Company as a whole, impressing as much as anyone else as being responsive to the call of Mr. Hall.

"The production taken as a whole is a great achievement: a staging in epic grandeur of Shakespeare glowing in genius and splendour.

"The important overall qualities of the production, which would not have been possible under anything but a long-term plan and settled conditions, are complete balance in atmosphere and performance; a sense of unity in aim and ambition; narrative swiftness and lucidity arising from common interest and integrity of purpose; and the force of performances that have an immediate effectiveness, individually and in relation to each other."

Bernard Levin in 'The Daily Mail' hailed it as "A production of epic, majestic grandeur, a landmark and beacon in the post-war English theatre," whilst Kenneth Tynan in 'The Observer' recognised the political lesson: "What we have at Stratford is gang warfare in armour. The great ones, almost to a man, are arrogant, savage and fickle; and so, aping them, are the common people, whose behaviour in Jack Cade's rebellion prompts the reflection that every Government gets the country it deserves."

Whilst calling it "superb theatre", James Arnott hailed the Company: "Gutted of irrelevances, the plays compel unrelenting attention and reward it richly by a number of performances of conspicuous merit."

All the cast were praised for their characterisation, interpretation and delivery. A number received particular note, especially the unknown David Warner as Henry VI.

"I have seldom witnessed such a finished performance by an actor who has barely started," wrote Kenneth Tynan.

B.A. Young in 'Punch' declared, "It is a beautifully-shaped performance that moves effortlessly to triumph," and added: "The sad young monarch, so sure of the power of good in a world where only evil prospers, yet so reliant on others for the strength to make a decision, is beautifully realised by Mr. Warner, and his death, where - a stroke of genius - he is made to force a kiss of forgiveness on murdering Richard's cheek, is a sublime end. This Henry is the archetype of every honest CND demonstrator who ever sat down in Trafalgar Square."

Peter Hall remembers "the effect David Warner had on an audience that didn't know who he was".

Alan Brien in 'The Sunday Telegraph' was delighted with York's three sons: "In the usual Shakespearean repertory, Edward IV is little more than a spear-carrier. Roy Dotrice plays him with all stops out - a lecherous, brutal, roaring whelp whose animal energy glows as hotly in his golden armour on the battlefield as naked in bed with his whore. Charles Kay's Clarence is ... an intellectual malcontent, an icily angry young prince, who can stab and swear with the worst of them. Ian Holm's Gloucester ... is a reasonable, winning personable boy, despite the withered hand, the buckled back and the club foot, whose acrid humour is expressed in deadpan politeness rather than sardonic snarls."

The 'Birmingham Post' critic J.C. Trewin wrote that Donald Sinden's performance "is for me the high event of these plays ... this York, for those with ears to listen, is an achievement altogether rare."

Brewster Mason's "velvet fox Warwick the Kingmaker" was hugely memorable. "To see the figure of Warwick loom up out of the smoke of battle and fall, alone in the centre of a dark, deserted stage, was to see the crumbling of man's earthly ambition."

Janet Suzman was applauded for "the historically doubtful but exciting Joan of Arc" and acted with "fanatical vigour". Suffolk, wrote J.C. Trewin, was "acted with the right insolence by Michael Craig".

"It was to be expected," said Alan Brien, "that Peggy Ashcroft would make Margaret a character far more human and interesting than the moaning old wind-machine that is all we usually get in 'Richard III'. She outfits her voice with a trilling

French 'r' which makes even the most conventional phrases both alluring and pretentious. She never goes limp when she has no lines or freezes like a waxwork when the spotlight is off her. At the reading of the marriage contract, she eliminates pages of text simply by a silent, debby smirk and shrug at the revelation that she has no dowry."

"It was Dame Peggy," recalls Roy Dotrice, "who pushed David Warner forward to take a special bow. I hadn't heard an audience respond like that to a performance since Peter O'Toole's Shylock in 1960."

Charles Kay remembers an amusing incident on the first night at the opening of the second half of 'Edward IV'. "The interval lights came down, and Ian Holm and I (as Richard and Clarence) entered from either side of the stage to acknowledge the newly crowned Edward IV. We turned up to the throne only to find it empty. No King. But the lights were up, we were there, and the audience were there. I cannot remember who initiated what followed, but not trusting ourselves to improvise the text, we indulged in two long whispering sessions, each culminating in a large guffaw of a somewhat hollow nature. Nerve-racked as we were it seemed to last forever, but at last, with great bravura, on came Roy Dotrice in a cloud of tobacco smoke, and the play was back on course.

"Later that night, I was in conversation in the theatre restaurant with actor Alfred Lynch who had been a member of the audience. Talking about the plays, he suddenly said, '... and that double secret joke between you and Richard ... that was riveting.'"

"The applause never stopped," remembers John Corvin. "After so many calls, we *had* to go. But, as we walked up the stairs to the dressing rooms, we could still hear the applause over the tannoy."

"It was so exciting, and incredibly euphoric," adds Ann Curtis. "At the end, the audience raised a cheer, which was a salute to adventure."

(Sc. 27, p. 1)

SCENE 27

(The Council Chamber)

(Enter KING HENRY, QUEEN MARGARET, PRINCE EDWARD, EXETER, OLD CLIFFORD, YOUNG CLIFFORD and SIR HUMPHREY STAFFORD)

KING: My lords,
Of all the cares that tend upon our crown
That which hath griev'd me most, until this hour,
Hath been that very instrument of order,
Which was devised for my chiefest comfort:
I mean, this council-board, which should have been
The prop and centre of our government;
But which, by cruel dissent and emulation,
Hath bred a thousand still-lamented sorrows
Within my kingdom and my unquiet soul.
Therefore, my lords, upon the Queen's advice,
To ease past ills and seek our future peace,
We have new-fill'd those places lately voided
By foreign absence or untimely death,
With such a kind of gentle counsellor,
As only is ambitious for our good.
Therefore we welcome you, good gentlemen,
Lord Say, Lord Clifford, and your valiant son,
And you, Sir Humphrey Stafford: welcome all.

ALL: Our love and duty to your majesty.

MARGARET: Have you no welcome for your princely son?

KING: In sooth, I have: most welcome, gentle Edward,
~~Our littlest councellor, but our best belov'd;~~
~~Thy promises are as Adonis' garden,~~

(Contd)

EDWARD IV: The opening scene with David Warner's annotations

EDWARD IV: Derek Smith (Jack Cade) Michael Murray (Stafford) *(National Geographic)*

EDWARD IV: David Warner (Henry VI) Donald Sinden (York)
Brewster Mason (Warwick) *(Gordon Goode)*

EDWARD IV: Donald Sinden (York) Charles Kay (Clarence)
Ian Holm (Richard) Roy Dotrice (Edward)
Peter Gatrell (Rutland) *(Geoffrey Wheeler)*

EDWARD IV: John Corvin (Clifford) Donald Sinden (York) *(Gordon Goode)*

EDWARD IV: Death of York. Clifford Rose (Exeter) Donald Sinden (York) Peggy Ashcroft (Margaret) John Normington (Young Clifford) *(Geoffrey Wheeler)*

EDWARD IV: Roy Dotrice (Edward IV) (*National Geographic*)

EDWARD IV: Susan Engel (Queen Elizabeth) (*National Geographic*)

EDWARD IV: Susan Engel (Lady Elizabeth Grey) Roy Dotrice (Edward IV) Charles Kay (Clarence) Ian Holm (Richard) *(Geoffrey Wheeler)*

EDWARD IV: Murder of Prince Edward (1964) Hugh Sullivan (Hastings) Derek Waring (Rivers) Alan Tucker (Prince Edward) Peggy Ashcroft (Margaret) Roy Dotrice (Edward IV) *(Gordon Goode)*

EDWARD IV: The Final Scene *(National Geographic)*

EDWARD IV: The Curtain Call *(National Geographic)*

# CHAPTER FIVE

Thursday, July 19 1963.

Two days after the triumphant openings of 'Henry VI' and 'Edward IV', the Company gathered in the Conference Hall to begin work on the third part of the Trilogy. Due to Peter Hall's illness in May, and the subsequent postponement of the first performances of the first two plays, almost two weeks had been lost in rehearsal time for 'Richard III'. So the advertised opening of August 13 was put back one week to August 20. Including Sundays, this gave them just thirty-two days.

''So,'' Hall urged, ''learn as fast as possible, because I don't want to throw it on in the last week in a great panic.''

He and John Barton, with Frank Evans, divided the twenty-three scenes between them, which allowed for double and, when the pressure intensified, treble rehearsals. To supplement the rehearsal space - when particular re-working on 'Henry VI' and 'Edward IV' was called - the Methodist Hall in Old Town and the Red Lion Inn on Bridge Street were used.

Continuing his highly-praised Richard of Gloucester was Ian Holm; Tom Fleming was Buckingham, Roy Dotrice continued as Edward IV and Charles Kay as Clarence; Susan Engel was Queen Elizabeth, Jeffery Dench played Derby, Hugh Sullivan as Hastings, Janet Suzman as Lady Anne, Derek Waring as Richmond and Dame Peggy Ashcroft completed her three-play rôle as Queen Margaret.

Hall explained the stage picture. ''After the sunny banners of 'Edward IV', we will have a terrible wedged-shaped window, as the throne room becomes a bunker. It is a very dark night of history, but not until we get to the interval do I want to establish the Fascist society, and have black leather for Richard's thugs.'' He emphasised that 'Richard III' was a far less complicated play than either 'Henry VI' or 'Edward IV', ''with much less table bashing''.

''We've put bits here and there, mainly as reference to the two earlier plays. Some work will be done on the scene between Elizabeth and Richard to illustrate the common sense of marriage being a rejuvenating process. We also wish to introduce Princess Elizabeth as a clearer explanation of the process of succession.

''We will start 'Richard III', not in an atmosphere of dark, but as we leave it in 'Edward IV' - sunny banners, a sunny society, and Richard still the young charmer. Then I want a processing of Edward's court from downstage to upstage in the throne room. But as they move, there's a brassy fanfare as at the end of 'Edward IV'. The throne room dissolves, the throne goes back, the walls go back, leaving Richard as the left figure in the procession; with his back to the audience, so he can turn round and say,

'Look at it, isn't it lovely? We've got peace with this dear son of York ... but not yet!'''

Referring to the opening performance of 'Edward IV', Hall continued: ''Something super happened on Tuesday night when Ian did his first soliloquy. The audience said, 'Oh, Richard III, funny, splendid, hurray!' and laughed. And then when he killed David, I felt in the house such a hatred for him, which lasted right through to the last scene. Now, if we can pick that hatred up at the beginning of 'Richard', we've got it made.

''Richard betrays the world of sanction, and many characters become absolutely demoralised to save their own skin. Everybody covers up, even to the point where those who have no need to, cover up. They cannot say what they think and *dare* not say what they know. The heart of the play is the study of power and the needs of power.

''It's fundamentally what Shakespeare is on about, every time he touches politics. That order is necessary, that it will always corrupt, that power always corrupts. In 'Richard III', there is a very strong sense of summing-up of past actions, of curses coming home to roost.''

Once again ''the Gospel according to Kott'' emphasised Peter Hall's reading of the play:

''The main scenes of 'Richard III' are unfolded on the lower steps, on the protagonist's way up. There is no tragedy of history without awareness. Tragedy begins at the point when the king becomes aware of the working of the Grand Mechanism. This can happen when he falls victim to it, or when he acts as executioner. These are the points at which Shakespeare carries out his great confrontations, contrasting the moral order with the order of history.

''Richard III compares himself to Machiavelli and is a real Prince. He is, at any rate, a prince who has read 'The Prince'. Politics is to him a purely practical affair, an art, with the acquisition of power as its aim. Richard III is not just the name of one of the kings who have mounted the grand staircase. Nor is he a collective term for one of many royal situations depicted by Shakespeare in his historical chronicles. Richard III is the mastermind of the Grand Mechanism, its will and awareness. Here, for the first time, Shakespeare has shown the human face of the Grand Mechanism. A terrifying face, in its ugliness and the cruel grimace of its lips. But also a fascinating face.

''In the last act of the tragedy, Richard III is only the name of a pursued king. The scene shifts from battlefield to battlefield. They are after him. He flees. He becomes weaker and weaker. They have caught up with him. Now he just tries to save his life:

'A horse! a horse! my kingdom for a horse!'

''So, this is how much all his efforts have been worth. This is the real price of power, of history, of the crown adorning the Lord's Anointed. One good horse is worth more than the entire kingdom. This is the last sentence of the great cycle of Shakespeare's historical chronicles.

"Richard ceases to be a clown only in the last act. Until then he affected outbursts of rage and fury, devotion, even fear. Now he is really afraid. Until now he had been the one to choose the part and stand above others. Now he is simply himself: a man whom they want to murder. Richard does not want to accept this part, but he must. He is not laughing any more. He is just a heavy, misshapen dwarf. Soon he will be butchered like a pig. From the head of the corpse the crown will be torn. A new, young king will now talk of peace. Rows of bars are lowered from above. Henry VI speaks of peace, forgiveness, justice. And suddenly he gives a crowing sound like Richard's, and, for a second, the same sort of grimace twists his face. The bars are being lowered. The face of the new king is radiant again.

"It is important for the audience to realise at the end," Peter Hall concluded, referring to the point he had made during his talk to the Company in April, "that Richmond's arrival is only a hopeful pause before the next tragedy. We can't believe that this is the answer."

"Those were ferociously busy rehearsals," remembers Jeffery Dench. "At times quite frenetic. We worked through the day, performed in the evening and rehearsed through the night. We were young then! Sometimes people just went to sleep where they stood. There was the time, it was about three in the morning, when Ronald Falk - dressed in storm-trooper uniform and monk's habit - went to sleep and fell from the top of one of the walls. Peter Hall was sitting two-thirds back in the stalls, and he reached the stage without his feet touching the floor. Later, again about three-thirty in the morning, we were working through one of the many technical rehearsals, so we were all in costume. Tom Fleming suggested 'a plate of porridge with cream. No one will notice'. So we put trousers over our costumes and drove to Hampton Lucy. When we returned, no one had noticed, and even our scene hadn't been reached."

It was also during these rehearsals that a gloriously apocryphal story swept through the Company. A great cricket enthusiast, Dame Peggy Ashcroft anxiously followed the Test Matches between England and the West Indies that summer. The legend was that she wore a small transistor radio underneath her chain mail and helmet, followed the match during performances and whispered the latest score to the assembled nobility.

The tension was often released inadvertently.

"Ian Holm was given a club foot, dagger, ugly mace on a chain, a withered arm and a huge deformed hump," recalls John Corvin. "John Barton had dreamt up the idea of a bottle-backed spider and suggested a huge goitre for Ian's hip. During rehearsal, Ian McCulloch as Ratcliff observed, 'The king is angry, see he bites his hip.' That put an end to the goitre."

Ian Holm told the 'Stratford Herald' earlier in the year: "I'm going to play Richard III for absolute sincerity. It's a great help to be acting him first as Gloucester in 'Henry VI' - it really takes the curse off Richard. Doing it this way, one gets the young man."

Later he explained the achievement. "I played Richard very much as a cog in the historical wheel, and not as an individual character, although that is inevitably how he emerged in the final analysis. It was always extremely difficult to play 'Now is the Winter' without already having established the relationship with the audience in the earlier play during the afternoon. When I played the young man, and joined in the fun with the other brothers in Dad's castle, I was then able to go through into the famous soliloquy very much with the feeling of greeting old friends again and saying 'Hi, here I am'."

He had reservations during rehearsals. "Although I was quite confident that I could do it, at the same time it had dangers, and it was an enormous responsibility. The other plays in the Trilogy had been a tremendous success, and people were saying that they couldn't wait to see 'Richard'. That was terrifying. Peter Hall saw this danger, and said that we would have to work hard at it to make sure it was a success. We tried very hard to get away from the Olivier/Irving image of the great Machiavellian villain. We did Richard as part of the Trilogy, and brought the other characters in the play very much more into perspective. So audiences would know who Edward and Margaret and Clarence were, and this made Richard a much more human character. I really don't think we could have done it the way we did it without the Company spirit that Peter Hall built up from 1960."

Ian Holm had been at Stratford since Peter Hall had arrived and - with John Barton - had established the Company style of speaking the verse. This was illustrated during a rehearsal on the stage of the scene between Richard and Lady Anne over the corpse of Henry VI. Sitting in the rear of the stalls, Peter Hall called out: "Janet, I can't hear you." Janet Suzman replied, "I'm speaking as loudly as Ian," to which Hall shot back, "Yes, but Ian's been doing it longer."

There was a further lesson as Janet Suzman remembers: "I could not understand how Lady Anne would be moved by this monster (Richard) who killed her father, killed her husband, and whom she loathed in every fibre of her being. At the end of the scene, how could she be at his knees, his for the asking? I went to Peter Hall who said, 'Don't ask questions. Just do it.' And he was right."

Ian Holm has said that he discovered things about himself whilst playing Richard, "All the cruelty and aggression in me came to the surface, and I was able to use it creatively for the character. I found myself going after effects that were jarring and abrupt - dynamic changes of pace and pitch, sudden sharp lunges of volume."

Jeffery Dench (who played Derby) remembers, "Ian would move his head from side to side like a snake as he slowly said 'Derby'". David Nathan in The Daily Herald remarked on this - "his head pecked back and forth like some carrion bird". "He told me," adds Jeffery Dench, "that he found it a very frightening part. One day he was seen in his garden throwing stones at the birds."

"I found it like climbing Everest. It was such a colossal engine, exploding on six barrels. There was no relaxation. It just went on, ploughing on bitterly to the end. And I ended the play with this colossal great battle, encased head to foot totally in black armour. Every conceivable weapon was hung on me from maces to swords to battle axes. It really was a physical and mental strain. At Chigwell School, all I learned was to throw a cricket ball eighty yards, but I developed a very strong right arm. So I was delighted to be the only person who could wield one of those great two-handed swords with one hand.''

The opening performance consolidated the success of the first two plays in the Trilogy. The audience's reception was ecstatic and the whole cast spontaneously joined them in applauding Ian Holm - ''He was such a very popular member of the Company,'' says David Warner - ''It was the most moving thing that had ever happened to me,'' Holm said afterwards.

The enthusiasm was reflected in the critical notices. Herbert Kretzmer in 'The Daily Express' recognised ''a smiling psychopathic killer in the grip of an advanced paranoia, an obsessed madman who sees himself the victim of numberless persecutions and anxieties''. Dennis Barker wrote, ''Richard plotted like a child, left with nothing to do on a rainy day. 'Gosh, I'm fed up - I'll find a cat and pull its tail'. Later this approach takes on a macabre quality of its own. It is pursued through to Richard's whimpering, sulky death at the hands of Richmond. The demand for a horse became a wail for a donkey ride.''

Holm's Richard, in the view of the 'Nottingham Guardian Journal', was ''a cynical little grunt. He plays the part as a mixture of a born actor and a successful psychologist. Tears and laughter come easily to him. He embarks on a series of murders almost light-heartedly. He is always sure of other people's reactions. When he achieves a good phrase - such as 'the blind cave of eternal night' - he is obviously pleased with it''.

Alan Brien in 'The Sunday Telegraph' enjoyed ''His acrid humour expressed through a mask of deadpan politeness rather than through sardonic snarls''. This was similarly picked up by Roger Gellert in 'The New Statesmen': ''Ian Holm makes something quite frightening of Richard. He has a quiet, secret, almost sexual delight in his own wickedness.''

''The choice of Ian Holm - short, boyish, pleasant faced - reflected the whole philosophy of the production,'' said Alan Brien. ''When every prop and every confrontation is designed to dwarf him, his midget monarch develops an insect insanity which scarifies us like the sight of an ant with his feet on the button of the H-bomb.''

Bernard Levin in 'The Daily Mail' applauded Ian Holm's fulfilment of a promise: ''...his humour is that of a man who knows his own strength and can afford to laugh at others' weakness; his voice is under beautiful and expressive control almost throughout.''

Gerald Barry in 'Punch' considered Holm's performance ''wholly fascinating''. ''...he plays all his soliloquies in gloating colloquy with the audience...(he) develops into the subtle and penetrating embodiment of a power-crazed psychopath, fearful alike of enemies, friends and self, as much victim as monster, who in the end goes berserk.''

'The Stratford Herald' called it ''a bold, imaginative and truly magnificent production''. R.B. Marriott in 'The Stage': ''Hall's production makes the play inevitably part of the human flow and dramatic progress of the earlier parts. But the production also stands as one of the richest, most clear and compelling interpretations of 'Richard III' in many years.''

For Bernard Levin ''the production has taken Shakespeare's Tudor propaganda and ennobled it with the sweep and majesty, the solidity and colour of true history''. Writing over twenty-five years later, Roger Lewis in 'Stage People' remembered ''an eager villain, a troll King''.

There were several dissenting voices. Peter Roberts in 'Plays and Players' considered that the chance to crown the two earlier productions had been ''frustratingly muffed'', whilst David Nathan - though swept along by the production - questioned the validity of the jolly villain: ''Fear, the real fear that should be felt in the presence of evil is absent.'' J.C. Trewin emphasised the same point: ''He terrifies people on the stage, but that is not the same thing.''

However, 'Richard III' was the completion of the Trilogy, and this significance was discussed by Eric Shorter, Dennis Barker and, in the 'Observer', by George Seddon who wrote, ''Curiously, the most self-contained play, 'Richard III', gains most from being made one of three. It then becomes, as the director Peter Hall says in his programme foreword, 'The retributive culmination of a struggle for power, its principal character not the splendid Machiavellian entertainer of stage tradition, moving nimbly in a welter of wailing ladies and inexplicable barons, but embodying in his own anarchic self, a judgement on the country that he rules'.''

This was reinforced on Thursday, August 22 (interestingly, the anniversary of the Battle of Bosworth, although few in the audience would have known), when all three plays in 'The Wars of the Roses' were performed together on the first Trilogy Day: 'Henry VI' at 10:30 am, 'Edward IV' at 3:00 pm and 'Richard III' at 7:30 pm.

All those associated with the production remember especially that first Trilogy Day. The extraordinary exhilaration, the amazing togetherness of the Company, the enormous excitement, the energy and the numbing tiredness.

''It was ecstasy,'' remembers Nicholas Selby. ''People queued all night; we felt deeply privileged.'' For David Warner there was ''a joy at doing something unique''.

And it *was* unique. Marathons, trilogies and all day performances have subsequently become an acceptable part of the theatrical calendar, but in 1963 the idea was new, exciting and adventurous. It caught the mood of the time, it was daring, it captured the public's imagination. W.A. Darlington, writing in 'The Daily Telegraph', said that to see the three parts in one day ''is a tough adventure (and) yields very little as a test of sitting power to the Passion Play at Oberammergau''.

J.C. Trewin in 'The Birmingham Post' acknowledged the gain in watching characters develop. "In such an extended venture as this we can hear and mark the maze of linking references that tie the chronicles together by steel threads."

George Seddon in 'The Observer', believed that the production was best seen in this way, "even though one emerged from it sagging with physical and emotional exhaustion".

J.W. Lambert in 'The Sunday Times' appreciated the preservation of Shakespeare's double vision, "of life as an evolving process and as a meaningless jangle, of kings as tyrants and as tired men, of the common people as both suffering human beings and as an insensate mob ... In the torchlit, ironclad, clamorous shadows of John Bury's set, a thousand imaginative strokes in direction and acting give an astonishing life to these groping brutes and the few men and women of vision among them."

Bernard Levin was definite. "Mr Hall and his Company, in the ten hours' traffic of their stage, have not only given us a production to remember all our lives; what they have done above all is to demonstrate that great drama, interpreted by men of imagination and understanding, has a power, and a reality that can make us forget entirely that we are in a theatre."

Writing later, Harold Hobson of 'The Sunday Times' believed, "The tremendous cycle carries the cheering message that other ages, given the chance, were as vile as our own. The world is not, as one might have supposed, getting worse; it is merely refraining from getting better. But our own time, it is true, has no such pattern of ineffectual beauty as Henry VI to redeem it."

Thirteen years later, Sheila Bannock in her article 'John Barton's 97 ways of doing Shakespeare' considered, "apart from the intrinsic creative quality, these productions swept clean away all the Victorian and later accretions of chauvinism, of the adulation of military glory, of selective romantic, heroic or anti-heroic interpretation of theme and characters which, until then, had almost hidden Shakespeare's plays from view. Some people protested at what they considered to be an irrelevant 'Brechtian' interpretation of the plays, apparently unaware of the fact that in many aspects they were, so to speak, putting Mother Courage's cart before the Shakespearean horse. Shakespeare's political and social vision in these plays was utterly removed from, often quite opposed to, that of Brecht, and these productions brought that out. If there was a valid comparison, it was in the dramatic style, in which Shakespeare had used alienation techniques much subtler than those of Brecht, and from which indeed Brecht had derived some of his own."

Before the performances, Peter Hall had given a bottle of champagne to each member of the Company, and later that Thursday evening they celebrated at Avoncliffe, where records of The Beatles thundered on well into Friday morning.

"It was a terrific moment," recalls John Corvin, "when Dame Peggy declared that we were all part of the finest hour of the Royal Shakespeare Company."

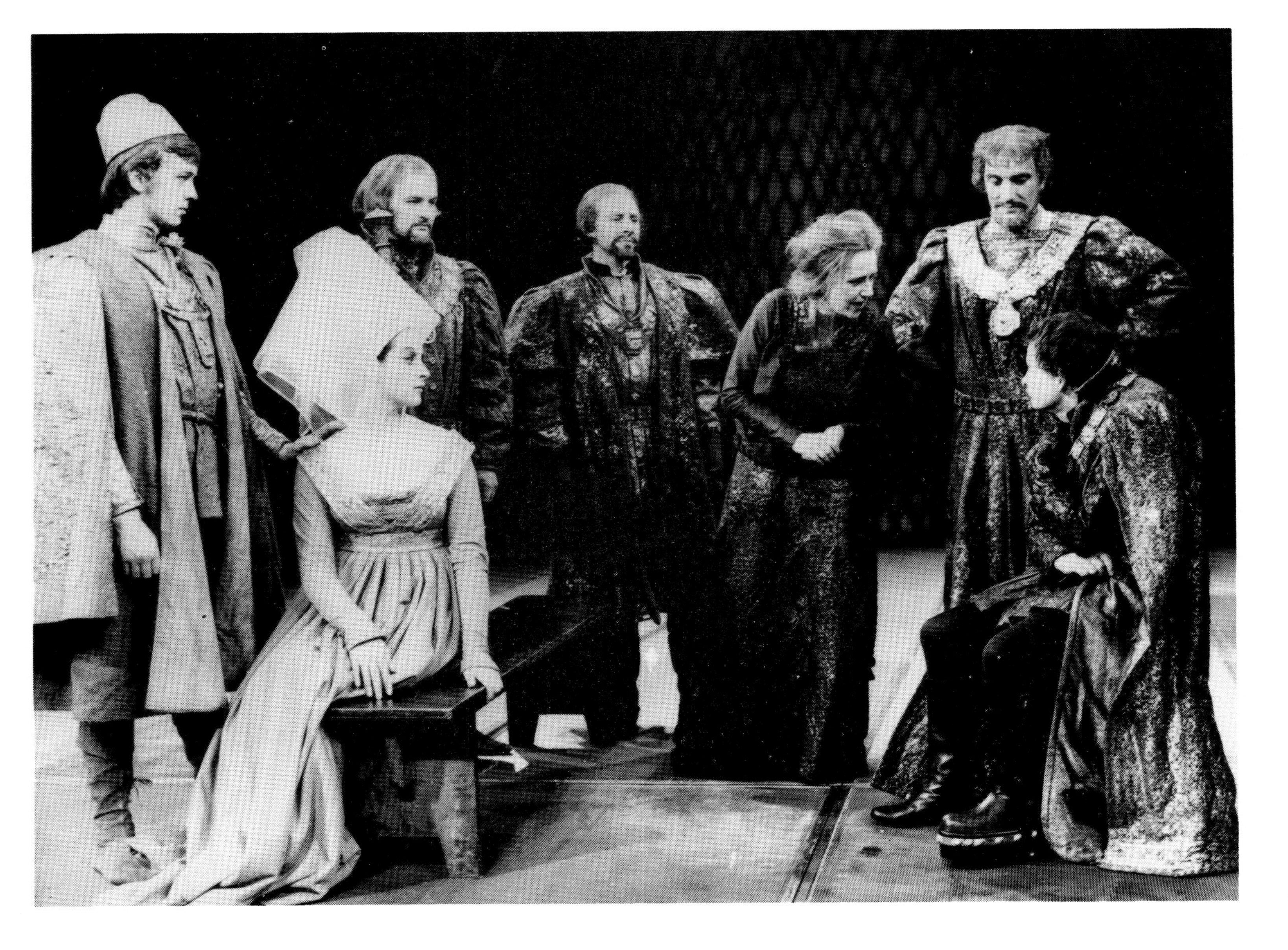

RICHARD III : Roy Marsden (Rivers) Susan Engel (Elizabeth) Hugh Sullivan (Hastings
Jeffrey Dench (Derby) Peggy Ashcroft (Margaret)
Tom Fleming (Buckingham) Ian Holm (Richard) *(Gordon Goode)*

RICHARD III: Roy Marsden (Rivers) Roy Dotrice (Edward IV)
Ian Holm (Richard) Susan Engel (Elizabeth) *(Gordon Goode)*

RICHARD III: Ian Holm (Richard) Tom Fleming (Buckingham) *(Gordon Goode)*

RICHARD III: Penelope Keith (Mayor's Wife) Ken Wynne (Lord Mayor)
Tom Fleming (Buckingham) Ian Holm (Richard) *(Gordon Goode)*

RICHARD III: Ian Holm (Richard III) *(Stratford Herald)*

RICHARD III: Ian Holm (Richard III) William Squire (Buckingham) *(Stratford Herald)*

RICHARD III: Janet Suzman (Queen Anne) *(National Geographic)*

RICHARD III: David Hargreaves (Norfolk) Ian Holm (Richard III) John Corvin *(Ratcliff)* *(Gordon Goode)*

**RICHARD III: Derek Waring (Richmond) Ian Holm (Richard III)** (*GordonGoode*)

Practising for the Charity Cricket Match. August 1963. Janet Suzman, Susan Engel, Peggy Ashcroft, Cherry Morris *(Birmingham Post and Mail)*

Peter Hall at the end of the final performance of The Wars of the Roses. November 14 1964.
*(Stratford Herald)*

## CHAPTER SIX

Dame Peggy Ashcroft's love of cricket showed itself in many forms during the summer months of 'The Wars of the Roses'.

The Test Matches between England and the West Indies were fiercely fought affairs. On the final day of the Second Test in June, rehearsals for 'Edward IV' were stopped, as any of four possible results could be resolved only with the last ball.

Michael Craig tells of members of the 'Henry VI' company gathered in the Conference Hall around Dame Peggy's transistor radio, as Trueman took six wickets in a twenty-four ball spell for only four runs in the Third Test. Even John Barton forsook his texts on this occasion.

During performances, Roy Dotrice, Charles Kay, Nicholas Selby, Clifford Rose and Jeffery Dench each remembers going on stage with the latest score and the responsibility of passing it along the line.

Then on Sunday, September 1, Dame Peggy organised a special 'Wars of the Roses' cricket match in aid of the World Freedom from Hunger Campaign. It was held at the King Edward VI playing fields on Manor Road, with Dame Peggy and Cyril Washbrook captaining the Lancastrians, and Donald Sinden and Sir Len Hutton the Yorkists.

Commentators were J.B. Priestly and Neville Cardus, and the neutral umpires included Brewster Mason and John Barton (dressed as Shakespeare). The ladies in the Company sold souvenirs and tea, and Leslie Caron presented the prizes.

''Dame Peggy strode out to the wicket wearing her crown,'' recalls Michael Craig, ''and when she was bowled out for sixteen by Sir Len, executed a beautiful stage collapse, and had to be carried back to the pavilion on a stretcher.''

David Warner scored six ''and then was hit on my dagger hand''. Ian Holm fielded complete with club foot and hunch back, and was accompanied to the wicket by Charles Kay as his sword carrier and runner. The RSC Wind Band played a fanfare each time a player went to the wicket or was out.

Susan Engel recalls padding up with great difficulty. ''There I was with Sir Len Hutton, one of the greatest cricketers of all time, and I couldn't work out how to do up a pad. 'Don't worry love,' he told me in broad Yorkshire, 'yesterday I was given tickets for the afternoon and evening of 'The Wars of the Roses', and I slept through it.''

Sir Len Hutton retained fond memories of the day. ''I finally got to meet J.B. Priestley at his home in Alveston - although he wouldn't let me use his billiard table. But the match was great fun.'' Penelope Keith kept a record of the score, and no one argued when she announced a draw.

It was also a profitable success, with £4,000 collected for the charity.

The productions of 'Henry VI', 'Edward IV' and 'Richard III' were unqualified successes, and performances were packed out with many people returning over and over. Tickets for the all day Trilogy were in great demand: "It became the popular 'in' thing to do," says Donald Sinden.

Some members of the audience would camp out around the theatre to buy the few standing tickets available, and roar the cast on from 10:30 in the morning until 11 at night. A young Ben Kingsley was so enthralled with Ian Holm's Richard III, that he walked back and forth in the standing area as Holm did likewise on stage, and finally collapsed with the tension.

"A taxi driver said to me, 'I never realised that Shakespeare could be like that'," Roy Dotrice remembers. "I think that was Peter Hall and John Barton's great service."

"Everything had such a wonderful buzz," is Cherry Morris' memory. "After the full day Trilogy, we were ready to do a midnight matinée. There was an unbelievable excitement in the dressing rooms. The plays, the Trilogy days, the Company and the audiences all made it an incredible experience."

"We really did feel that we were making theatrical history," says Jeffery Dench, "and it was all such fun. A quite extraordinary time. In the years since, when I have acted in many parts of the country and often with younger actors, I have been known as 'the one who was in 'The Wars of the Roses'." This was an experience shared by many.

"The plays covered a vast canvas," Brewster Mason remembered. "I found the whole experience fascinating. When the plays came off the page, the wonderful parade of characters was a compelling sight. And then there were all those alarums and excursions, and swords and banners and smoke. In the full sweep of performance, one had to be careful not to have one's head cut off in reality. Also there was no escaping the semblance of reality - my armour, with the addition of a replica of Warwick's sword, weighed 78 lbs. So actors do have mundane problems apart from agonising over the soul of the play."

"There was a great deal of blood, sweat and tears, and sometimes it all seemed utterly impossible," recalls Charles Kay. "The coat hangers cracked and fell under the strain of the costumes. The wings were littered with sweaty actors, and huge bottles of cologne were lined up in the back dock. But morale could not have been higher!"

Martin Jenkins explains the diversity needed by many members of the Company. "During the course of the three plays, each spear-carrier probably died at least six times. I expired several times for both the Lancastrians and the Yorkists. One had to die carefully as the wire-mesh floor cut into the skin very easily. Feigning dead, with great heavy boots dashing around within inches of your face, took some concentration. I also disliked riding the big upstage walls. These were positioned either side of the stage and could be swung in to alter location. We were meant to perch precariously on a very narrow ledge (hidden from the audience) and, looking fiercely 'butch', remain bolt upright as the walls were moved into place. Occasionally, if operated by over-enthusiastic stage hands, the walls would move with lightning speed, and it took all one's powers of balance to remain upright. I always admired Peter Geddis who actually volunteered to fall off one of these walls during a battle."

"I played 'The unknown soldier of the Battle of Orleans' in 'Henry VI'," explains Peter Geddis. "One night I was nearly killed, when through lack of concentration, I fell and landed on top of Shaun Curry ("It looked very good from the front," thought Jeffery Dench). Anyway, it upset the rhythm of the way I was to land, and I was knocked out. Evidently I was carried from the stage and I regained consciousness in the Conference Hall. I was furious with myself, and Shaun was furious too. Not because I had fallen on him but because, whilst a doctor was checking him over, someone played cards for him in a game of poker in the Green Room, and lost his hand and his money."

For Martin Jenkins, "the battles were great fun but dangerous. None of us were properly trained, but John Barton egged us on enthusiastically, so we swung our huge broadswords with great gusto, hacking and cutting without really knowing what we were doing. I found these fight sequences alarming because without my glasses I could see no more than ten feet in front of me. My opponent would hiss instructions to me: 'Step a little left, now lunge'."

Ann Curtis remembers there was a terrifying rehearsal when the lighting cues got out of sync, and a whole battlefield was suddenly black. "Peter yelled from the stalls to stop, but couldn't make himself heard above music and sword clangour. Eventually, the lights came up, and there was every soldier where he was meant to be; the battle having continued perfectly disciplined in the darkness."

The following extract from the Availability Chart is for six scenes in 'Henry VI', and illustrates the furious activity backstage during performances, as actors changed their allegiance with a surcoat or tabard and shield.

| | | | |
|---|---|---|---|
| Scene 10: French Soldiers | - | Ronald Falk | James Falkland |
| | | John Corvin | Brian Harrison |
| English drum | - | Peter Geddis | |
| English colours | - | Tim Wylton | |
| Scene 11: York Soldiers | - | Martin Jenkins | Tony Boden |
| | | Tim Nightingale | David Rowlands |
| | | David Hargreaves | Henry Knowles |
| Scene 12: Somerset Soldiers | - | Roger Jones | John Walsh |
| | | Marshal Jones | Robert Jennings |
| Scene 13: Talbot Soldiers | - | Peter Geddis | Tim Wylton |
| | | David Rowlands | John Steiner |
| | | Roger Jones | John Walsh |
| | | Marshal Jones | Robert Jennings |

| | | | |
|---|---|---|---|
| French Soldiers | - | James Falkland | John Corvin |
| | | Ian McCulloch | Roy Marsden |
| | | Brian Harrison | |
| Scene 15: York Soldiers | - | Robert Jennings | Shaun Curry |
| | | Martin Jenkins | Tim Nightingale |
| | | David Hargreaves | Tony Boden |
| | | David Rowlands | Henry Knowles |
| French Soldiers | - | Ronald Falk | James Falkland |
| | | Roy Marsden | Brian Harrison |
| | | Ian McCulloch | |
| Scene 17: English Soldiers | - | Martin Jenkins | Roger Jones |
| | | Tim Nightingale | David Hargreaves |
| | | John Steiner | Henry Knowles |
| French Soldiers | - | Robert Jennings | Tim Boden |
| | | Peter Geddis | Tim Wylton |
| | | David Rowlands | John Walsh |

As Martin Jenkins has explained, the many battle scenes in 'Edward IV' necessitated similar quick changes as the opposing armies of Lancaster and York swept across the stage. It required concentration and a good memory in the darkened backstage, as actors fought for space amongst the racks of costumes and weapons.

"We had to be quick on our feet," says John Corvin, "and the stage management made sure that we returned a shield to the right rack and a tabard to the correct rail. The pace was frantic, but the great Company spirit sustained us."

It was this spirit that helped when the unexpected happened, as Cherry Morris recalls. "I understudied Dame Peggy as Queen Margaret, and one evening in late October when I had a night off, I went out for dinner with my husband-to-be Michael Murray - who was also in the Company, playing the Earl of Oxford. I arrived back at my flat to find a note from Frank Evans, saying that Dame Peggy had slipped on some wet leaves, fallen and hurt herself, and would be off for all the three plays for several days. I was allowed to call which actors and what scenes I liked, in order to rehearse the next morning. Although I was nervous, at the same time I felt very confident. I had studied the text diligently and watched a lot of rehearsals. Nevertheless, I stayed up all night and Mike heard all my lines. But the thing that really buoyed me up was the Company itself: all the actors and stage staff who gave me great encouragement and stimulation - even to whispering stage directions to me. After the matinée performance, Donald Sinden invited me to his house in Tiddington, where his wife opened a bottle of wine and prepared omelettes."

Cherry Morris played Margaret for eight performances from October 31 to November 9 inclusive, and it was Patrick Donnell, the RSC's General Manager, who then told her that she would play Margaret later at the Aldwych, when Dame Peggy left the cast.

'Richard III' was the production on Friday evening, November 22. Peter Hall was at the performance, "as a matter of routine, seeing that it was in a healthy condition. It was also my birthday so, although I was working, I was hoping for a relaxed evening."

Tom Fleming (playing the Duke of Buckingham) heard the news of President Kennedy's assassination on a radio in his dressing room. Stunned, he told others as they waited in the wings. Susan Engel heard during the performance: "I came on to announce the death of Edward IV - 'My Lords, the King is dead'. And I remember looking out at the audience at that point and thinking, 'They don't know that Kennedy is dead'."

"In the interval," adds Peter Hall, "the news spread among the audience. The artificial sense of evil on the stage seemed now to correspond with a sense of evil in our own lives. I never remember a blacker atmosphere in a theatre. The second half of Shakespeare's chronicle of blood and violence seemed unbearably true to human behaviour."

Due to end on November 30, the season was extended one week until December 7 for extra performances of 'Henry VI', 'Edward IV' and 'Richard III'. As the season closed several articles appeared, presenting critical overviews and appraisals of the Trilogy.

Charles Marowitz - who had assisted Peter Brook on the RSC's 'King Lear' in 1962, and had observed rehearsals for 'The Wars of the Roses' - declared, "What emerges most clearly from this continuous action is a kind of running battle between primitive instincts and man-made order, with the id destroying more than the super-ego ever builds."

Robert Kee, writing in 'Harper's', said: "The success of the production is a 'total' one in the sense that it is the result of indistinguishable interdependence between direction, skilled adaptation, design and acting - and above all between actor and actor, so that there are no stars in the old bad sense, or, alternatively, they are all stars... The total success would have been less without the clarity of Peter Hall and John Barton's narrative line. The strength of this clarity has been absorbed almost magically by each actor and actress so that each character is, in a way, quite exceptional for a Shakespearean production; individual, subtle and complete."

Peter Roberts, in 'Plays and Players', similarly commended the text: "Peter Hall's production and John Barton's edited version of the plays have the three virtues of Faith, Hope and Clarity. The Faith and Hope stem from the belief and optimism in the ability of the original plays to hold a modern audience. John Barton's editing of the plays in consequence is no ham-fisted bowdlerisation, but a delicate piece of reconstruction involving some perfectly executed invisible mending, in which Shakespeare is deftly patched with Shakespeare and any loose ends that might result from trimming are consequently carefully threaded into the narrative flow... But of these three virtues, Faith, Hope and Clarity - Clarity is the greatest."

J.C. Trewin: "The splendour... is in its speed and surge. It thunders down upon us in a vast cataract. It causes us to realise, yet again, the futility of any academic discussion of Shakespeare that does not relate his plays to the theatre."

Claudia Cassidy, writing for 'The New York Times', was impressed by the scope and the concept: "The instant you enter the theatre, the Cycle takes possession...a grim, gray, shadowy and highly suggestive single setting, part mailed fist, part ancient chapel... The staging moves swiftly and clearly, so that even in the maze of traitors and turncoats you have no trouble following the gory paths of Lancaster and York. The battle scenes are merciless, handling those fearful weapons with the skill of what can only be merciless practice. The performance is extraordinary, both in quality and vitality."

W.A. Darlington in 'The Daily Telegraph' concluded, "...because so much of them (the original plays) consist of bustling action, they do act a great deal better than they read... As 'The Wars of the Roses' develop to their full peak of horror, the characters seem to lose some of their individuality and sink back once more into their background of promiscuous slaughter. Henry, the only man in the whole pack with anything like a conscience, continues to waffle feebly while all about him heads are rolling and corpses are being cleared away... and hatred runs riot... One's feeling when the carnage is over is relief!"

'The Times' applauded Peter Hall for revealing Shakespeare's early political vision. "Peter Hall has managed to secure a style of playing in which the public rhetoric, with which the characters dispute their political ends, is counterpointed against their private ambitions and desires. And beyond the personal level, the characters seem to be in the grip of a spell which hurries them on helplessly from one blood-soaked disaster to the next. It is the view of history as the operation of fate: the curse on the House of Lancaster, and not to be removed until the accession of Richmond. This view we may regard nowadays as superstitious; but the way in which it is worked out shows Shakespeare as a greater political realist than in the later Histories, where isolated characters are given more scope to influence events."

1964 was Shakespeare's Quartercentary year, and an all-day presentation of 'The Wars of the Roses' opened the Royal Shakespeare's commemorative season at the Aldwych Theatre in London, on Saturday, January 11.

Taking John Corvin to the theatre, a taxi driver exclaimed, "You're not going to believe this, but they're opening a theatre at ten o'clock in the morning!" As at Stratford, 'Henry VI' began at 10:30am, 'Edward IV' at 3:00pm and 'Richard III' at 7:30 pm.

"In the morning," wrote J.C. Trewin in 'The Birmingham Post', "some of the audience attempted rather coyly to make a party of it during the interval, and to talk about staying power and breaks for food. But archness disappeared. During the afternoon one heard only of the performance and of the shaping and development of the linked histories."

Because the Aldwych stage was smaller than that at Stratford, the productions had to be re-staged and the set squeezed in. The backstage area was also much less, so when the great walls of the set swung back, access to the stage was restricted to narrow corridors. Martin Jenkins recalls, "Some of us took to 'opting out', especially at the matinée performances of the battle of Tewkesbury, simply to avoid being maimed. It was also the time of the London power cuts, and we all dreaded a power failure when we were busily slashing away at each other."

Also, due to the London Fire Regulations, Tony Watts' splendid flaming torches made of sheep gut and tallow, which had blazed at Stratford, were replaced. One new feature which speeded the production was the diamond-shaped council table. At Stratford it had been carried on and off, but at the Aldwych it rose smoothly from the floor.

"Except," says Roy Dotrice, "during the opening performance of 'Edward IV' there was some technical malfunction and a group of us sat around waiting for the vast Council table to rise in order to begin the scene. It didn't, so I just got on with the scene, and strolled over to where the table was. I think everyone expected me to suddenly rise in the air as the table appeared."

Michael Craig remembers another amusing incident on that opening day. "When the great walls swung back and the throne came down its track, and all the Lords in full dress awaited David Warner's entrance, we noticed that someone had left an 'Evening Standard' and a cup of tea on the throne, which was anachronistic to say the least. I don't think David saw the offending objects until he was about to sit on them."

The invention of a Barton-like line saved an awkward moment in 'Henry VI' when Janet Suzman as Joan lunged at Derek Waring playing the Dauphin. The blade of her sword fell off. Improvising quickly, Janet roughed up the Dauphin, but was stopped by John Corvin bringing his halberd between the two and crying, "Forbear your hand upon the King!"

Once more, the actors enjoyed an unqualified triumph. "After the matinée of 'Edward IV'," recalls Nicholas Selby, "Donald Sinden, Michael Craig and I went to the Garrick Club to celebrate, and we enjoyed a liquid evening. We returned to the theatre at 10:45pm to join the full curtain call, putting a long cloak over our day clothes, and swayed happily. Michael, who shouldn't have been in charge of a pram, drove us all home across Blackfriars Bridge."

Critics once more hailed "the extraordinary sense of ensemble and the overpowering total design showing the work as a divine comedy of God's revenges".

R.B. Marriott, writing in 'The Stage' about the remarkable clarity, rhythm and flow of the Aldwych production, said, "At the Stratford opening last year they seemed rich and stirring, but now they have even greater dramatic impact."

B.A. Young in 'The Financial Times' applauded "the most majestic and exciting spectacle''. Frank Cox in 'Plays and Players' greeted the production as ''a theatrical miracle''.

Once again, as at Stratford, the Trilogy was the hottest ticket in town, and audiences roared and stamped.

There had been several changes in the cast. Clive Swift now played Talbot, Michael Craig doubled his Suffolk with a rousing Jack Cade. Martin Jenkins replaced Ken Wynne as Lord Say and, from February 15, Cherry Morris took over from Dame Peggy Ashcroft as Queen Margaret. Tom Fleming and Clifford Rose joined the RSC's World Tour of 'King Lear' and 'The Comedy of Errors' and their parts were played respectively by Paul Hardwick as the Duke of Buckingham and Donald Burton as the Duke of Exeter.

Donald Burton recalls how he was invited to join the production. ''As a student at RADA, I had admired a commemorative book about the 1951 Histories at Stratford, and the actors involved who had been able to carry a character through as many as three plays. My regret then was that, in all probability, such a programme would never be mounted again. Many years later, while appearing at the Bristol Old Vic, I was asked to take over a part for a transfer from Stratford to the Aldwych in something called 'The Wars of the Roses'. Having been very busy, I had not even heard of the production. The part was the Duke of Exeter, and featured in the first two plays in the Trilogy. Here was something very near that of which I had been so very envious. I was told I had better see the productions before beginning rehearsals - so dutifully I went to Stratford.

''Never before - nor indeed since - have I been so overwhelmed in the theatre. From the opening moment...and consistently throughout the nine or so hours of what seemed to be history itself unfolding, the impact was staggering. This was the greatest thing I had ever seen on any stage. And I was going to be part of it.''

The three plays had a nine week season at the Aldwych Theatre, during which there were three Trilogy days.

At the same time the Company began rehearsals for the first three productions of a sequence of seven History plays - culminating in 'The Wars of the Roses' - which were to be presented at the Royal Shakespeare Theatre in 1964 for Shakespeare's 400th anniversary.

Some of the original members of the company had other commitments and left. Replacements included Paul Hardwick as Humphrey, Duke of Gloucester, William Squire as the Duke of Suffolk and the Duke of Buckingham, Eric Porter as Richmond, Donald Layne-Smith as Reignier and Lord Say, Colette O'Neil as Eleanor of Gloucester and Lady Bona and Clive Swift as Jack Cade.

Clive Morton was cast as Lord Talbot in 'Henry VI'.

''He felt the ambivalence of being in the Company,'' says David Waller, ''but also a great delight.''

Waller himself came from the Belgrade Theatre in Coventry. Peter Hall had invited him after seeing a performance of 'The Caucasian Chalk Circle' directed by the young Trevor Nunn.

"I was very tense being with that company at first, particularly as I was new to the production. My lasting memory is of supporting Clive Morton, dying as Talbot, and his armour cutting into my arm and the wire mesh floor cutting into my knee."

There was also re-casting. Derek Waring now played Rivers, Jeffery Dench was Sir Humphrey Stafford, David Hargreaves played Norfolk, John Corvin was Ratcliff and Philip Brack played the Duke of Somerset.

Rehearsals began at the beginning of the third week in June, and although John Barton has said that "the plays were economically rehearsed because they came at the end of a very heavy season" (Richard II, Henry IV Parts 1 and 2, and Henry V had preceded them), there was nevertheless substantial restaging and 151 alterations to the text.

Changes included a scene between the Dauphin, Joan and Burgundy in 'Henry VI', which had been cut in 1963 and was now restored. It included an exchange between Joan and Burgundy, which was part original Shakespeare and part John Barton:

Joan: *What dost thou seek to gain by thy revolt?*
*Who join'st thou with, but with a lordly nation*
*That will not trust thee but for profit's sake?*
*If Talbot thrives, then thou art Talbot's pawn:*
*If Charles triumphest in despite of thee,*
*Farewell to all thy power and policy.*
*If France is one and England in dissent,*
*How easily may France regain its own.*
*Look on thy country, look on fertile France,*
*And see the cities and the towns defac'd*
*By wasting ruin of the cruel foe.*
*Behold the wounds, the most unnatural wounds,*
*Which thou thyself hast given her woful breast,*
*One drop of blood drawn from thy country's bosom*
*Should grieve thee more than streams of foreign gore.*
*Come, come, return; return, thou wandering lord;*
*Charles and the rest will take thee in thy arms.*

Burgundy: *Either she hath bewitch'd me with her words,*
*Or nature makes me suddenly relent.*
*Forgive me, country, and sweet countrymen:*
*My forces and my power of men are yours.*

Joan (aside): *Done like a Frenchman: turn and turn again!*

In 'Edward IV', the scene where York and Warwick storm the palace of Henry VI and York sits on the throne was greatly rewritten, and there was much significant cutting and transposition in 'Richard III'.

During the spring of 1964, the Royal Shakespeare Theatre Club was formed to encourage theatregoing and stimulate new audiences, and Club performances preceded the official opening nights: for 'Henry Vi', Wednesday, July 29; for 'Edward IV' (which the Duke of Edinburgh attended) and 'Richard III', the matinée and evening performances on Wednesday, August 12.

The sequence of three plays ran fourteen times, one of which closed the season on Friday and Saturday, November 13 and 14. Unlike the 1963 and Aldwych seasons, there were no Trilogy days in 1964.

Frank Cox wrote an appreciation of the restaged cycle in 'Plays and Players' under the title 'In Full Bloom'.

"The production as before is packed with things to stand up and cheer about, and now gains more cohesion through some ironic casting links with the other plays in the repertory. King Henry's despairing admission at the height of the conflict with the rebellious York - 'I know not what to say, my title's weak' - has an added poignancy now since David Warner himself plays the wronged Richard II as well. Donald Sinden's York again rises to the painful grandeur of that blood-soaked death scene. Chained to two crossed spears and punctuated by the taunting chuckles of Dame Peggy's Queen Margaret, he plumbs a level of such choking intensity in the final speech, that when at the first performance the vital paper crown toppled from his head, the weary kick with which he rejected it could only turn the mishap into an advantage ... Warwick's business-like survey of the field at the end of the battle of Towton is a master stroke ... (And) who last year would have dared to predict that Ian Holm, in a rôle which was indisputably Olivier's, would this year come close to making it his own.

"In a programme note Peter Hall speaks of 'the intricate pattern of retribution, of paying for sins, misjudgements, misgovernments'. These points are rammed home by magnificent acting by casts that tackle their heavy tasks with unflagging zeal. They leave one with unforgettable pictures."

'The Times' admired the restaging of particular scenes, "of which the most striking is the drum-head trial of Joan of Arc, which has been removed from the battlefield to a stately chamber where Warwick and York, goblets in hand, play sadistically with the wretched girl before sending her to the stake."

Bamber Gascoigne in 'The Observer', noting the cast changes, added, "It is a measure of the Company's strength that the tone of the original has been in no way blurred."

"I can think of nobody more suited to Talbot than Clive Morton," wrote John Gardner in 'The Stage'. "His distinctive style is hand-made for the blood-and-guts, king-and-country Field Marshal cracking his jingoistic way... William Squire... tremendous subtlety as Suffolk and sugar-coated cyanide as Buckingham... Paul Hardwick is most perceptive as Gloucester, his deposition was the most moving few minutes."

"There was a feeling of great confidence in the Company in 1964," says John Corvin. "There's nothing like success, and the reception for those three plays was always overwhelming. There was great spirit in the Company, although it was a demanding season - there were three matinée days, on Wednesday, Thursday and Saturday. But it was Shakespeare's anniversary, and we played to record audiences of near one hundred per cent capacity."

"It became a way of life," remembers Ann Curtis. "With nine performances a week, and so much connected activity, we couldn't think beyond those productions. They really were all-consuming."

There were amusing moments. Janet Suzman losing a contact lens during the seige of Orleans, and asking people in the next scene to look out for it - on that vast Stratford stage - which some actually did. Chris Williams and Gavin Morrison toppling into the Avon on their way to a performance, and rushing into the theatre, into costume, and onto the stage as two very wet French soldiers.

"And the quite wonderful moment," recalls Roy Dotrice, "in the Coventry scene in 'Edward IV' when Brewster Mason announced to the assembled army - and to the audience in the theatre - that 'I am the Bod, the Heady and the Limbs of Lancaster'. Brew was probably aware afterwards that he had said it, but he was a disciplined actor. Those lucky enough to have our backs to the audience collapsed."

And there are other memories.

"I held a spear," says James Laurenson, "and had one line: I told them that Orleans was ta'en and the Duke of Bedford dead. Paul Hardwick waved his hand at me, and that was my moment."

Stephen Hancock, playing the Clerk of Chatham in 'Edward IV', had a real fear when the halter was placed around his neck. "Clive Swift as Cade had so much danger about his performance."

John Corvin felt the same about Ian Holm. "I knew that I was in the presence of a great actor. I came to my moment with my contribution to the scene, and I can assure you that I was riveted to the spot. Ian's Richard was the embodiment of evil. I watched him carefully. I never took my eyes off that man, but directed the thought. That was the frightening atmosphere Ian instilled."

The realistic and disturbing sound of beheading was achieved by the off-stage amplification of a sliced cabbage. Members of the audience reacted in different ways, so the St. John's Ambulance Brigade were in attendance at performances of 'Edward IV'.

John Russell Brown in 'Shakespeare's Plays in Performance', reviewed the violence in the productions: "The plays became a high class cartoon, a relentless horror comic...horror and violence were presented by liberal splashes of blood, and by inventive business that elaborated every opportunity for the exhibition of cruelty and pain that the text suggested...Joan of Arc cut her own wrist like a Tamburlaine with a very large sword; Young Clifford's head was cut off on stage and carried around upon a spear; Clarence was drowned in the malmsey-butt at the back of the stage, rather than 'within' as the words of the text direct." Subsequently, during the television recording of the scene, Charles Kay nearly drowned in the process. "In the Paper Crown scene, the cruel humour of the lines was played close to hysteria. When Margaret stabbed York it was with a quick movement, and then she wept. Then the tears stopped with a wild, painful cry. In this scene the violence was emphasised as much as anywhere, but there was also rhetorical and musical control and a daring, emotional performance revealing depths of unwilled and conflicting desires."

Ted Valentine, who played the Lieutenant of the Tower in all three plays, remembers the transformation of Dame Peggy. "She was a young giggly girl when it was a 'Henry VI' performance, but she would sit alone in the Green Room on 'Richard III' days and grumpily push her coffee cup aside."

"It all had to do with preparation," Dame Peggy explained. "The old hag could go on in half an hour, but it took at least an hour to make up the youthful part. You have to be meticulous when you want to look your best."

Fulbright scholar Robert Potter recalled "a young girl...conveying with body language the graceful uncertainties of a seventeen-year old - not unlike the unforgettable Juliet of Margot Fonteyn".

For Donald Burton, the Histories of 1964 were the realisation of his earlier ambition. As Exeter, he appeared in all seven plays - even coming on stage at the very end of 'Richard III', "as a sort of benediction", which the character had not done in 1963.

Finally, for the eighteen-year-old Tim Pigott-Smith, it was the most thrilling time. "The 'Wars of the Roses' were triumphantly under way, and the Quatercentenary made Stratford as a town a focus for the world. I was awaiting my A-level results, so was odd-jobbing for the great John Collins in the Paint Shop, and on occasions was able to work on the enormous paint frame high above the back of the stage. From this vantage point I could observe the final rehearsals on stage. I shall never forget the thrill of the armies sweeping on and off the great stage as the huge periaktoi swung into place and the kettle-drums pulsated. The energy that surged up from that space was colossal. There was no question of failure: the atmosphere was positive, driving, electric."

The Royal Shakespeare Company in 1964 enjoyed what Peter Hall called "a happy and friendly deal with the BBC to televise a certain amount of our productions". John Barton's anthology 'The Hollow Crown' and the Clifford Williams production of 'The Comedy of Errors' had already been seen under this arrangement.

Because of the extraordinary success of 'The Wars of the Roses', the BBC decided on a new and exciting approach to the transfer of the stage production to television.

In July 1964, the BBC producer Michael Barry went to Stratford to watch the final Theatre rehearsals, so that he could listen to the directors and absorb the thinking that lay behind the instructions they gave. This was followed by discussions with two television directors - Robin Midgley and Michael Hayes - at which Peter Hall and John Barton led a scene-by-scene review.

Michael Bakewell, Head of Plays for the BBC, explained the problem they had set themselves. "From the outset, all those concerned were intent on finding a new way of presenting Shakespeare on television .. to re-create a theatre production in television terms - not merely to observe it but to get to the heart of it, to find out what it was that made this particular production so remarkable.

"The possibility of moving the whole production into a studio was rejected at a very early stage. Although this would have given us total control from a television point of view, it was felt that the theatre for which the production had been designed played an essential part in the undertaking. This was not merely a human problem but a technical one. The solution seemed to be to convert the Royal Shakespeare Theatre into a television studio, to dispense with an audience and to adapt the stage so that our cameras could involve themselves as deeply as possible in the action.

"The heart of the production was the set - John Bury's iron cage with its revolving periactoids, trundling throne, council board and descending grilles. The whole conception of the plays had been worked out precisely in terms of this and to attempt to re-create the sets in the studio would be futile. There was also the added advantage that if the production was recorded at Stratford we would have the whole cast at our disposal for rehearsals while they were still performing in the theatre, rather than interfering with an already overloaded schedule by obliging the actors to commute to London.

"What was needed at Stratford was to give the cameras exactly the kind of freedom and mobility they would enjoy in the studio, so half the seats in the stalls were removed, the apron was enlarged so that it pushed right out into the auditorium as a 'thrust' stage and a vast wooden platform was erected across the stalls area for the cameras and sound booms to manoeuvre on. Eight cameras were used, including a special Japanese hand-held camera which could penetrate right into the battle scenes. A tower was built at the back of the stage, so that a camera could overlook the top of one of the periactoi to give a view over the walls and on to the men beneath. Another camera was installed in a pit at the front of the stage to give a kind of death's-eye view. And an additional two hundred lights were brought in."

"The production had been mounted for a proscenium stage," says Donald Sinden, "but for television the audience, through the camera's eye, could actually enter into the action. To this end, the semicircle of scenery could be assumed to continue round, forming a complete circle. In fact it did not, so each scene had to be shot twice."

"What has been most interesting to me," said Michael Barry at the time, "and has added enormously to our ability to get on quickly with this difficult job in a short time, is the fact that we have a permanent company here, whose life is centred in this community."

"The way in which they were able to adapt themselves - at a time when they were playing nine long and demanding performances in the theatre - to rearrangement for the television version has been quite amazing. It was inspiring to see the confidence and sureness of a company used to working with each other in unison. If they were tired - which they must have been - it never showed in their performances.

"Before the theatre finished the season they were giving nine performances a week, while we were concurrently rehearsing them from 10 to 5 (or on matinée days from 10 to 1). We were changing their positions and their groupings and the nature of some of their expressions - yet they went back and gave those vigorous performances every night. Even so, it was not unusual at around six o'clock to see some part of that evening's play being given a refurbishing run-through."

The text remained untouched. "We wouldn't have presumed to touch it," explained Michael Hayes, "but we naturally had to re-stage quite a bit. The big sort of wide-screen scenes, for instance, could not be done on television. The long shots would have reduced Dame Peggy to about a quarter of an inch. You couldn't catch everything for the screen: those wonderful Council scenes - so marvellous and full of rich acting, everyone within his own character. But with the camera you just had to miss so much.

"The television departed a long way from what was seen on the Stratford stage, but it conveyed overwhelmingly the feeling of the action. As in so many moments in the operation, it was found that the most successful way of conveying the spirit of the Hall and Barton production was not to imitate what they had done but to achieve the same aim by doing something that would prove much more effective in television terms. A fundamental difference between theatre and television staging is involved in the problem of depth and perspective. A great many scenes had to be re-staged and re-angled to make this possible, but again this only served to convey the strength and solidity of the original.

"One of the great achievements of the Stratford production was to make real people out of a succession of barons who can all too easily become a series of abstract and bewildering place names,. Television was able to tie in absolutely to this concept by presenting the whole conflict and intrigue in close-up."

"Scaling-down was essential, not only in terms of the action itself but in the size of the actors' performance," continued Michael Bakewell. "Actors accustomed to filling the whole of the Royal Shakespeare Theatre had to rethink their performance in relation to the accusing eye of a television camera often only inches away. This turned out to be admirably suited to the characters of York, Warwick and Gloucester who were continually planting information, letting the audience know what they intended to do next... They (were) talking directly to us, which is, after all, the basic point of the soliloquy."

John Barton believed, "The plays were packed with soliloquy and they worked better on television than in the theatre."

For Peter Hall, that was a lesson for the future. "The ability of the camera to intensify the dialogue between the actor and the audience, which you get in the theatre - particularly in soliloquy and complex verbal passages when the camera can get in very close - made the intricacies of the thing more intimate and more human. I think that this is the way to do Shakespeare on television, with the ability to convey subtleties. The closer you shoot, the more the words mean.''

Due to the length of the complete production, the plays were divided into sections of approximately fifty minutes in length, and the television directors worked on alternate sections:

| Play | Scenes | Director |
|---|---|---|
| Richard III | 55 to 58 | Michael Hayes |
| | 60 to 68 | Robin Midgley |
| | 70 to 77 | Michael Hayes |
| Henry VI | 1 to 9 | Robin Midgley |
| | 10 to 18 | Michael Hayes |
| | 19 to 26 | Robin Midgley |
| Edward IV | 27 to 35 | Michael Hayes |
| | 36 to 44 | Robin Midgley |
| | 45 to 54 | Michael Hayes |

The central problem of production was to re-create as fully as possible the experience felt by the audience watching the plays at Stratford, and it soon became apparent that this could not be done simply by slavishly photographing the action. Theatre has its own grammar and television another. They are involved in different concepts of reality and illusion. One of the great features of the Stratford production was the movement of the set itself: the periactoid swung around to become at one moment the walls of harfleur, at another the council chamber in London; the background grilles would fly up and the great throne would be trundled forward; the council table would rise up from its slot in the forestage - none of this, it was realised, would work on television. This was partly a question of reality, but was more so one of tempo. Michael Bakewell further explained that a television audience expected the cut, fade, and mix, ''and the ingenious movement of John Bury's set would, in the end, have become merely tedious.'' A regrettable decision.

Following the close of the season, the Company returned from three free days to begin the television work. For contractual reasons, 'Richard III' was recorded first, between November 20 and 27. 'Henry VI' was recorded between December 1 and 8, and finally 'Edward IV' between December 11 and 18. It was believed for many years that the recording had been lost, but in 1988 a copy of the videotape was acquired by the library at the Shakespeare Centre in Stratford-upon-Avon.

The three productions were shown on BBC television on successive Thursday evenings between April 8 and 22 1965, and later on national television in the United States and Canada.

"It was very poignant to hang up the costume for the last time," remembers John Corvin. "To finally end that great adventure which had begun twenty-one months before."

Writing at the end of 1964, Peter Hall considered the achievement. "The great success of 'The Wars of the Roses' history trilogy comes from their heavily ritualistic pattern; fathers kill sons and sons kill fathers, and we are forced to experience the passionate responsibility of mother to son, of king to country, of people to king, of blood to blood. Political intrigue is supported by instinctive passions, and there is no doubt of retribution for every wrongdoer.

"These history plays with their bloody heads, brutal carnage and sense of fate were not appreciated by the nineteenth century. This is not surprising, it was hoped then that such horrors were past. We know now that this optimism was premature.

"I believe that Shakespeare is still a very living and contemporary force, and it is our duty to reinterpret the plays in live modern terms. That is why I think it is sometimes permissible to cut and adapt as we have done with 'The Wars of the Roses'. And if the purists object, this is not a police state. The plays are still there after we have finished mucking about with them - us or anybody else. They haven't been suppressed. And in ten years time, people will look at our work and say, 'That was dreadful' because it won't speak to them as the work speaks now. And they'll do their own adaptations, their own productions, their own interpretations."

# APPENDIX 1

## THE WARS OF THE ROSES Company 1963

Dame Peggy Ashcroft
Barbara Barnett
Tony Boden
Jolyon Booth
Philip Brack
John Corvin
Michael Craig
Shaun Curry
Valerie Cutts
Jeffery Dench
Roy Dotrice
Susan Engel
Ronald Falk
James Falkland
Tom Fleming
Peter Geddis
Anthony Gatrell
Peter Gatrell
David Hargreaves
Brian Harrison
Ian Holm
James Hunter
John Hussey
Brian Jackson
Martin Jenkins
Robert Jennings
Marshal Jones
Roger Jones
Charles Kay
Penelope Keith
Henry Knowles
Rhys McConnochie
Ian McCulloch
Roy Marsden
Brewster Mason
Caroline Maud
Lee Menzies
Cherry Morris
Michael Murray
Tim Nightingale
John Normington
Clifford Rose
David Rowlands
Nicholas Selby
Donald Sinden
Derek Smith
John Steiner
Hugh Sullivan
Janet Suzman
Madoline Thomas
Phillipa Urquart
David Walsh
Derek Waring
David Warner
John Welsh
Tim Wylton
Ken Wynne

## APPENDIX 2

### THE WARS OF THE ROSES Company 1964

Dame Peggy Ashcroft
Katharine Barker
Tony Boden
Philip Brack
Murray Brown
John Bruce
Donald Burton
Jessica Claridge
Bruce Condell
John Corvin
Elizabeth Croft
Jeffery Dench
Michele Dotrice
Roy Dotrice
William Dysart
David Ellison
Susan Engel
Peter Forbes-Robertson
Carl Forgione
Peter Gale
James Garrett
Peter Geddis
Guy Gordon
Sheila Grant
Terence Greenidge
John Hales
Stephen Hancock
Paul Hardwick
David Hargreaves
Ian Holm
John Hussey
Marshall Jones
Maurice Jones
Stanley Lebor
Andrew Lodge
David Lyn
Fergus McClelland
Rhys McConnochie
John Malcolm
Paul Martin
Brewster Mason
Lee Menzies
Gareth Morgan
Gavin Morrison
Clive Morton
David Morton
Colette O'Neil
John Normington
Michael Pennington
Eric Porter
David Quilter
Michael Rose
David Rowlands
Michael Sarson
Nicholas Selby
Donald Sinden
William Squire
Deborah Stanford
Hugh Sullivan
Janet Suzman
John Cargill Thompson
Charles Thomas
Madoline Thomas
Alan Tucker
Ted Valentine
David Waller

Roger Jones
Charles Kay
Henry Knowles
James Laurenson
Donald Layne-Smith
David Warner
Derek Waring
Malcolm Webster
Chris Williams
Tim Wylton

# APPENDIX 3

| HENRY VI | | PROP LIST | OP Side |
|---|---|---|---|
| Furniture: | preset | French Bale ass (*) | |
| | | Winchester curtains | |
| Wings | Cart and top and small bale, pole and sword. | | |
| | Mortimer chair and poles | | |
| | Lancaster banner | | |
| | 2 ladders set up (smallest on top) | | |
| | Bedford pennant | | |
| | Steel bench | | |
| | 2 steel stools | | |
| | French throne | | |
| | French chair | | |
| | Brass table | | |
| | Council table | | |
| | 2 cannon (weighted) | | |
| | Gloucester bed and pillow and two sheets and blanket | | |
| | Winchester bed and large pillow and cover | | |
| | Maddie's mat (zodiac signs) | | |
| | Simpcox stool, cross and crutch | | |
| | 5 torches and 3 brackets | | |
| | 2 staves | | |
| Props | 4 papers Scene 4 | | |
| | 2 large papers 3 small papers Scene 17 (sealed) | | |
| | 2 firing pins | | |
| | Small map | | |
| | 2 council table papers | | |
| | 2 bloody cloths | | |
| | Metal axe | | |
| | Mirror | | |
| | Blood | | |
| | Mud | | |
| | 2 whips | | |
| | Dauphin shield | | |
| | Burgundy shield | | |

As the audience looks at the Stratford stage, the Prompt side is on the right.

* 'ass' means 'the Assembly area' - a particular Stratford term, refering to the area in front of the proscenium.

HENRY VI SETTING LIST PROMPT side

| | |
|---|---|
| Preset | Coffin cloth and four candles, trestle, 2 banners each truck. |
| | U/S seige wagon and box and small sword and fighting dagger. |
| | Joan sword to dressing room |
| | Papers to Winchester, Warwick, and 2 to Suffolk. |
| Wings | 2 French banners |
| | Reignier shield |
| | Alençon shield |
| | Joan banner |
| | 3 steel stools |
| | Steel bench |
| | 2 French chairs |
| | French throne |
| | 2 Gloucester chairs |
| | Gloucester table, stool, and staff |
| | Cart and Burgundy pennant on side |
| | Burgundy pennant |
| | Talbot pennant |
| | French pennant |
| | Burgundy banner |
| | Large and small bale |
| | 2 swords - Sinden and Mason |
| | 6 torches and 3 brackets |
| | Altar, 2 candles, curtain and head board |
| | 2 staves, chopper, axe and knife. |
| Props | Prayer book |
| | Paper for Kay Scene 15 |
| | Paper for Kay Scene 19 |
| | Paper for Warner Scene 14 |
| | Burgundy baton |
| | Quill |
| | 3 Coronation cushions |
| | Crown, orb, sceptre, ring, sword |
| | 2 whips |
| | Tray, jug and 2 goblets |
| | Miniature of Margaret |
| | 2 purses |
| | Falcons |

Suffolk head in shirt
Mirror
Blood
Mud
Reignier map
Exeter baton
Helmet and armour on strap

HENRY VI RUNNING LIST OP Side

| | |
|---|---|
| Scene 4 | Set Mortimer chair in prosc |
| Scene 5 | Set cart U/S Strike Mortimer chair |
| | Set bench and 2 stools prosc |
| Scene 7 | Set small French throne in prosc |
| | Check clear for strike of 2 carts |
| Scene 8 | Strike bench and stool in ass |
| | Strike 2 stools prosc |
| | Set French pike U/S |
| | End of scene strike 2 carts |
| Scene 9 | Set 2 cannon |
| | Fill 2 torches |
| | Collect Talbot pennant P/S |
| | End of scene strike throne ass. |
| Scene 13 | Set bench ass. |
| | Stand by prosc with 2 bloody cloths and mirror for Talbots |
| Scene 15 | Strike bench U/S |
| Scene 16 | Set brass table prosc |
| | Set French chair ass. |
| Scene 17 | Set Gloucester bed U/S made up |
| | INTERVAL |
| Strike | French furniture |
| | Set bench prosc stool ass. |
| Scene 19 | Set 3 stools prosc |
| | Set bench and stool ass |
| | Collect black baton from P/S |
| Scene 20 | Fill torch and bracket |
| | End of scene, light torch |
| Scene 21 | Check Simpcox stool, cross and crutch |
| Scene 22 | Set bench and 2 stools prosc |
| Scene 24 | Prepare Gloucester bed in ass. |
| | Fill 3 torches |
| | Strike Gloucester bed |
| | Fill 2 torches, set on wall |
| | Set Winchester bed U/S |
| Scene 25 | Strike Winchester bed U/S |

EDWARD IV | PROP SETTING LIST | OP Side

Furniture

Stafford banner
French chair
Jumbo sword
Large sword
Large Richard sword preset in ass
Warwick banner
Clarence banner
Lancaster banner
4 gold banners
Large Warwick shield
Clarence shield
Hastings shield
Somerset shield
Norfolk shield
Heavy Clarence shield
2 York death spears
French stool
Exeter baton
Tower table
2 Tower stools
Sinden head (preset truck)

Props

Stafford baton
Corvin scroll
Mason paper
Black baton
2 whips
Menzies scroll
Bloody napkin
3 letters Scene 45
6 tearable papers Scene 46
2 pairs manacles
Prayer book
Bible
Cross
York death chain

EDWARD IV SETTING LIST PROMPT Side

Preset Stage 4 steel stools 2 steel benches
Throne Council Table
Ass. Hobby Horse
Quick change - 3 Dotrice shields Gold sword
Silver sword Blanket

Rostra on truck
U/S Cade Cart and barrel and rope Armour 2 spades pick small axe hoe bale head (facing d/s)

WINGS
2 Cade banners
York banner
York shield
Jumbo shield
Loot for cart (and banner armour 2 crosses horn 4 candlesticks)
French throne
French stool
Buckingham banner
Tatty Lancaster banner
Drum and sticks and strap
8 torches
Small Warwick shield (preset in ass)
Cade dagger
Warcart and York pike in back and pole and bucket on side
Barrel
Small bale
Long spear
Bale and chain
2 bundles
2 crossbows and 2 bolt boxes
mattress
3 square lanterns
Buckingham Shield
Margaret Shield
2 Lancaster pikes
4 Talbot pikes
6 York pikes

PROPS

- Henry prayer book
- Cade sickle
- Round horn
- 4 French loaves
- Cabbage in cloth
- 2 pairs of manacles
- 9 goblets (1 wooden Cade)
- Jug
- 4 bottles
- Black purse
- Warwick ring
- Paper Dame Peg Scene 31
- Paper Crown
- Clifford head
- Brace of birds
- 3 tearable papers
- Oxford paper Scene 49
- Water bottle and loop and cork
- Baby
- Blood
- Mud

RICHARD III SETTING LIST PROMPT Side

| | |
|---|---|
| Ass. | Edward V council table |
| | Steel bench |
| | Steel stool |
| | 2 candlesticks |
| U/S | Malmsey butt |
| | Mortimer chair with poles |
| Wings | Black bier and cheesepiece and rope and black bedspread |
| | Cart |
| | Cart and full top |
| | 4 cannon |
| Prop Table | Manacles |
| | Bucket of water |
| | Cardboard bucket |
| | 2 iron jugs |
| | 2 beakers |
| | Plate of food |
| | Box with 2 leeches |
| | Leather Bible |
| | Inkwell and quill |
| | Ledger |
| | 4 torches and brackets |
| | Basket and napkin |
| | 2 stool tops |
| | Small bale |
| | 4 water bottles, one with cork and strap |
| | Candlestick and candleholder |
| | 8 large candles |
| | Very large sword |
| | Pennant |
| | Ratcliff shield (grey and grey rat) |
| | Norfolk shield (green and 3 black crosses) |
| | Richard's black helmet with crown |
| | Richard's black armour, arm and glove |
| | Richard's fighting dagger |
| | |
| | 2 firing pins |
| | 1 blood capsule |

2 gold Coronation banners
York banner (grey and white rose)
Lancaster banner (red roses on red)
Richmond banner (white and green and red dragon)
Richard banner (grey and white boar)
Derby banner (grey and 3 yellow stags heads)
Norfolk banner (green and 3 black crosses)
Letter for Queen Elizabeth
3 flasks of liquid nitrogen
Blood
Mud

| | |
|---|---|
| Scene 55 | Help Clarence with manacles |
| | U/S after Clarence entrance set Mortimer chair |
| | after Hastings' entrance set bier |
| | tie Warner to bier, cover, hand blood capsules |
| Scene 56 | Ass. set steel bench |
| | Collect 2 coronation banners from OP banner rack to PS banner rack |
| Scene 57 | Collect R Jones' monks hood, set OP prop table |
| | U/S set bucket of water on stool plus 6 straws |
| | U/S check malmsey butt set |
| | fill torch |
| Scene 58 | Stand by to light torch for 1st Murderer |
| | U/S stand by to take torch from Lieut. of Tower |
| | Ass. check steel bench set |
| | U/S stand by for water noises, strike bucket, stool and straws |
| | U/S stand by for strike of malmsey butt |
| Scene 59 | Check tower table and 2 tower stools collected from OP. |
| | Ass. light 2 candlesticks |
| | Stand by to upend steel bench |
| Scene 62 | Pros. Stand by to take stick from Hastings |
| | Stand by to hand small candlestick to Hastings |
| Scene 64 | Ass. Stand by to help with Council Table, Steel bench going on in Scene 65 |
| Scene 65 | Take axe to OP, collect plate of food, bring to PS |
| | Fill 3 flasks with liquid nitrogen |
| | Ass. Set Tower table plus 2 Tower stools with wooden tops, ledger, inkwell and quill |
| | Fill 4 torches with brackets |
| | Fill Iron jug with Lucozade |
| Scene 66 | Ass. Upend steel bench |
| | INTERVAL |
| | Pros. Set steel bench |
| | Strike malmsey butt to back of wings |
| Scene 67 | Stand by to light 4 torches with brackets |
| Scene 70 | Collect Richard's crown and helmet from OP table |

| | |
|---|---|
| | to PS prop table |
| Scene 72 | Ass. Stand by to hand ledger and inkwell and quill<br>Clear steel bench into wings |
| Scene 73 | Ass. Set candleholder with lighted candles, iron jug and beaker, Richard III fighting dagger, black armour arm and glove<br>Ledge near Pros. Check inkwell and quill there, set paper<br>Pros. Stand by with crown and plate of food. |
| Scene 74 | U/S 3 carts ready to go on<br>Pros. 2 cannons (facing backwards) set |
| Scene 76 | Standby to light ghosts candles<br>Take white rose banner from PS banner rack to OP banner rack<br>Norfolk's sword and shield in wings PS set OP near winch<br>Position cannon near Pros<br>Position cannon (not practical) near U/S<br><br>After ghost sequence:<br>U/S Stand by to put Richard's dagger in his scabbard<br>Ass. Check tower table and stools struck to the very back<br>Collect crown, fix to helmet and stand U/S to hand to Ratcliff<br>U/S Help with cannon<br>Pros. Help with cannon<br>Stand by on top of wall to throw 2 flasks of liquid nitrogen<br>Take flask of liquid nitrogen to O/P<br>Stand by to strike cannon at end. |

| | |
|---|---|
| Scene 55 | Ass. Stand by for strike of Mortimer chair. |
| | Set steel bench |
| Scene 56 | U/S stand by for strike of bier |
| Scene 57 | Set bier with black cheesepiece, black cushion and Edward IV cover |
| | Check Holm puts dagger to O/P prop table for Rose. |
| | Check Holm's dresser hands him a Warrant |
| | Pros. After Margaret's exit, set Tower table plus tower stool and mattress |
| | Ass. Strike steel bench (leave it in Ass.) |
| Scene 58 | Pros. Stand by strike of tower table, 2 tower stools, mattress |
| | Tower table plus 2 tower stools to P/S |
| Scene 59 | Ass. Light 2 candlesticks |
| | Stand by to upend steel bench (crowd exit) |
| Scene 60 | Pros. After exit of crowd set bier, cover Edward |
| Scene 61 | Stand by strike of bier and 4 candlesticks |
| Scene 63 | Pros. Set 2 steel stools |
| | Ass. set steel bench and steel stool |
| Scene 64 | Set 3 pieces of iron U/S |
| Scene 65 | U/S Stand by for iron sound effects |
| | Ass. Stand by to upend steel bench |
| | U/S Strike 3 pieces of iron |
| | INTERVAL |
| | U/S Strike council table to conference hall, sweep up broken pieces |
| | Pros. Set steel bench |
| | Ass. Passageway - set Talbot pennant, bucket of water plus towel |
| | Tray: Black leather map, inkwell, quill, paper, iron jug, iron beaker, candleholder with 6 inch candle |
| | Fill 4 torches with brackets |
| Scene 67 | Stand by to light 4 torches |
| Scene 72 | Ass. Stand by to strike steel bench into wings. |
| | Light candle on tray |
| Scene 74 | Stand by to strike cart |

| | |
|---|---|
| Scene 75 | Stand by to strike 2 carts. Stand by for 2 cannons coming off in Pros. |
| Scene 76 | U/S Stand by with Richmond dress shield with small sword. Cannon going on.<br>Pros. Cannon going on<br>Collect 2 banners<br>Top of Wall - throw liquid nitrogen |

# APPENDIX 4

## THE WARS OF THE ROSES

## AWARDS

| | | |
|---|---|---|
| 1963 | Plays and Players London Theatre Critics' Awards | |
| | Best Director: | Peter Hall |
| | Best New Actor: | David Warner |
| 1964 | Evening Standard Drama Awards | |
| | Best Actress: | Dame Peggy Ashcroft as Queen Margaret |
| | Variety Club of Great Britain Awards | |
| | Best Stage Actress: | Dame Peggy Ashcroft as Queen Margaret |

# APPENDIX 5

## SCENE NUMBERS AND TITLES

April 1963

### HENRY VI

| Scene Number | Title |
|---|---|
| 1 | Westminster Abbey |
| 2 | 1st Orleans |
| 3 | Gloucester v Winchester (cut in 1963 and never restored) |
| 4 | Temple Garden |
| 5 | 2nd Orleans |
| 6 | 1st Tower (Scenes 5 and 6 were transposed) |
| 7 | 1st Palace and Council |
| 8 | Rouen (called Burgundy in 1964) |
| 9 | 1st Paris |
| 10 | 1st Bordeaux |
| 11 | 1st Gascony |
| 12 | 2nd Gascony |
| 13 | 2nd Bordeaux |
| 14 | 2nd Palace (called 2nd Council in 1964) |
| 15 | 1st Anjou |
| 16 | 2nd Anjou |
| 17 | 2nd Paris |
| 18 | 3rd Palace (called 3rd Council in 1964) |
| 19 | 1st Gloucester's House |
| 20 | 2nd Council (called 4th Council in 1964) |
| 21 | 2nd Gloucester's House |
| 22 | Simpcox |
| 23 | 3rd Paris (this scene became Scene 29 in 'Edward IV') |
| 24 | 3rd Council (called 5th Council in 1964) |
| 25 | 4th Palace (called 6th Council in 1964, when Scene 25A, Suffolk Murder, was introduced) |
| 26 | Cardinal's Bedchamber (called Winchester in 1964) |

## EDWARD IV

| Scene Number | Title |
|---|---|
| 27 | 4th Council (called 7th Council in 1964) |
| 28 | 2nd Street (called Blackheath in 1964) |
| 29 | Flight to Kenilworth (this scene was cut and never restored. Scene 23 was placed here) |
| 30 | 3rd Street (called 1st Street in 1964) |
| 31 | Kenilworth |
| 32 | Dartford |
| 33 | Iden's Orchard |
| 34 | 6th Palace (called 9th Council in 1964) |
| 35 | 1st York (called Sandal Castle in 1964) |
| 36 | 1st Wakefield |
| 37 | 2nd Wakefield |
| 38 | Mortimer's Cross |
| 39 | 2nd York |
| 40 | 1st Towton |
| 41 | 2nd Towton |
| 42 | 3rd Towton |
| 43 | Scotland |
| 44 | 7th Palace (called 10th Council in 1964) |
| 45 | 4th Paris |
| 46 | 5th Council (called 11th Council in 1964) |
| 47 | Warwick |
| 48 | 4th Street (called 2nd Street in 1964) |
| 49 | 5th Street (called 3rd Street in 1964) |
| 50 | Coventry |
| 51 | Barnet |
| 52 | Tewkesbury |
| 53 | 2nd Tower |
| 54 | 8th Palace (called 12th Council in 1964) |

## RICHARD III

| Scene Number | Title |
|---|---|
| 55 | 6th Street (called Opening in 1964) |
| 56 | 7th Street (called Outside Tower in 1964) |
| 57 | 9th Palace (called Palace in 1964) |
| 58 | 3rd Tower |
| 59 | 10th Palace (called 2nd Palace in 1964) |
| 60 | 8th Street (called Street in 1964) |
| 61 | 11th Palace (called 3rd Palace in 1964) |
| 62 | 9th Street (called Outside Tower in 1964) |
| 63 | Hastings' House |
| 64 | Pomfret (called Rivers' death in 1964) |
| 65 | 6th Council (called 13th Council in 1964) |
| 66 | Baynard's Castle |
| 67 | 10th Street (called Outside Tower in 1964) |
| 68 | 12th Palace (called 4th Palace in 1964) |
| 69 | 13th Palace (called 5th Palace in 1964) |
| 70 | 11th Street (called 6th Palace in 1964) |
| 71 | 12th Street (called 7th Palace in 1964) |
| 72 | 13th Street (called 8th Palace in 1964) |
| 73 | Tamworth (this scene and Scene 74 were transposed) |
| 74 | Salisbury (called Buckingham Death in 1964) |
| 75 | 14th Palace (this scene was cut. It does not appear in the copies |
| of | the text given to the actors at the start of rehearsals) |
| 76 | 1st Bosworth |
| 77 | 2nd Bosworth |

Scene 8 was cut in 1963 and restored in 1964, with lines transposed to Scenes 2 and 9.
The character of Bevis was cut in 1964.
Scenes 43 and 44 were transposed in rehearsal.
The news of Henry's capture was transposed from Scene 44 to Scene 46 in 1964.

# APPENDIX 6

## COSTUME INVENTORY: MALE CHARACTERS

**TONY BODEN**

| | |
|---|---|
| *Basic*: | Grey noil with chain sleeves |
| *French soldier*: | Orange-brown tunic and helmet |
| *Burgundian soldier*: | Purple tunic, helmet with chain mail and blue flash |
| *Warwick soldier*: | Dark grey tunic and helmet |
| *York soldier*: | Light grey tunic and helmet |
| *Citizen*: | as Mob |
| *Mob*: | Brown-green undergarment, leather jacket, steel helmet and leather belt |
| Storm trooper: | Black tunic - padded, heel tips, armband, lump belt, helmet, chain gloves |
| *Abbey Solder*: | Blue-red tabard, metal collar, camail |
| *Richard III*: | Monk's hood |

**JOLYON BOOTH**

| | |
|---|---|
| *Reignier*: | Red-green jacket with high collar, White night shirt, hat, chain skirt, Gauntlets, slippers, boots, armour belt, armour legs, night cap |
| *Clerk of Chatham*: | Black gown with white collar, black hat, Belt, shoes, knee pads |
| *Bishop of Ely*: | Cap, gold underdress, red gown, cross and chain, red gloves, ruby ring, cape with hood, gaiters, Coronation cloak |
| *Mob*: | Off-white smock, Leather jerkin |

**PHILIP BRACK**

| | |
|---|---|
| *Duke of Burgundy*: | White shirt, purple padded tunic, belt, boots, chain gloves, hat, chain skirt, chain cuffs, collar, helmet, camail, gauntlets |
| *Norfolk*: | Lamé under shirt, brown-gold tunic, lump belt, chain of office, Brown tabard, Coronation gown, noile underbodice, dress belt, helmet, armour legs and arms, gloves and gauntlets, chain of office on calico |
| *Second Murderer*: | Dark grey under shirt, dark grey trousers, boots with side buckles, ragged scarf, felt jerkin, leather wrist bands, dagger, belt |

**JOHN CORVIN**

| | |
|---|---|
| *French soldier*: | Orange-brown tunic, helmet |
| *Basic*: | Grey noile with chain sleeves |
| *Mob*: | Purple-brown gown, brown cloak, leather belt, brown woollen hat |
| *Old Clifford*: | Basic under-bodice, Dark red tabard, Armour legs and arms, helmet, gloves, belt, mail collar, whip, sword and scabbard, red cloak, black gown, Red cooking gloves, chain of office, belt |
| *Citizen*: | Chain for Richard III |
| *Berkeley*: | Hat, black coat, belt, gloves |
| *Breton Officer*: | Brown leather tunic, Cloak, gloves, belt, helmet, boots |

**MICHAEL CRAIG**

| | |
|---|---|
| Suffolk: | Green lamé shirt, Green tunic, belt, Hat, gloves, cloak, green tabard, under bodice, armour legs and arms, gloves, helmet, armour belt, chain of office, coronet |

**SHAUN CURRY**

| | |
|---|---|
| *Basic*: | Grey noile with chain sleeves |
| *Lancastrian soldier*: | Red tunic, helmet |
| *Citizen*: | Green shirt |
| *Mob*: | Light brown underbodice, grey gown, belt, hat |
| *York soldier*: | Light grey tunic, helmet |
| *Talbot Captain*: | Leather tunic, armour legs and arms, lump belt, chain collar, helmet, cloak |

**JEFFERY DENCH**

| | |
|---|---|
| Bassett: | Lancastrian tunic, red gown, hat, gloves |
| *Ambassador*: | Blue-black gown, velvet hat, belt, gloves |
| *Keeper*: | Old suede boots, trousers, kilt with sleeves, leather jerkin, sheepskin shoulders, belt, plaid sash |
| *Lawyer*: | Black overgown, grey dress, hat |
| *Derby*: | Brown lamé shirt, brown tunic, hat, gloves, belt, tabard, armour legs and arms, lump belt, helmet, armour gloves, underbodice, brown gown, coronet |
| *Stafford*: | Shirt, red tunic, lump belt, black hat, gloves, red leather brigandine |

**ROY DOTRICE**

| | |
|---|---|
| *Bedford*: | Red-blue tabard, armour legs and arms, cloak, camail, knee pads, mittens |
| *Edward*: | Boots, chain mail tights, yellow floor cloth jacket, belt, yellow tabard, sword belt, silver armour legs and arms, gloves, helmet, belt, gold tabard, gold armour legs and arms, gloves, helmet, three crowns, shirt, dressing gown, death cap, gold and white tunic, white cloak, chain of office, belt, slippers |

**RONALD FALK**

| | |
|---|---|
| *Basic*: | Grey noile underbodice with chain sleeves |
| *York soldier*: | Light grey tunic, helmet |
| *Bevis*: | Green coat, cloak, rags, belt |
| *French soldier*: | Orange-brown tunic, helmet |
| *Doctor*: | Black hat, black gown, belt |
| *Lawyer*: | Black grosgrain gown, white collar, hat, gloves, belt, black boots |
| *Courtier*: | Green lamé shirt, green tunic, hat, chain |

**TOM FLEMING**

| | |
|---|---|
| *Buckingham*: | Heavy brown gown, two pairs of gloves, Belt, cloak, hat, chain of office, ghost shirt, silver lamé shirt, gold jacket, two small lump belts, gold tabard, noile undergarment with chain skirt, large lump belt, armour legs and arms, helmet with chain, gauntlet gloves, armour, sword, light gauntlets, belt, shirt and trousers for execution, Coronation gown, coronet |

**ANTHONY GATRELL**

| | |
|---|---|
| *Prince Edward*: | Travelling clothes and coronet |

**PETER GATRELL**

| | |
|---|---|
| *Prince Richard*: | Jacket, tights, cloak |

**PETER GEDDIS**

| | |
|---|---|
| *Basic*: | Grey noile with chain sleeves |
| *Lancastrian soldier*: | Red tunic and helmet |

| | |
|---|---|
| *York soldier*: | Light grey tunic and helmet |
| *Mob*: | Black hat, brown cloak, hood, oatmeal smock, piece of grey material |
| *Storm Trooper*: | Black padded tunic, lump belt, armband, helmet, gloves, heel tips |
| *Talbot soldier*: | Khaki tunic, helmet with chain and orange flash, gauntlets |
| Son who killed Father: | Camail |

**DAVID HARGREAVES**

| | |
|---|---|
| *Basic*: | Noile grey with chain sleeves |
| *Falconer*: | Feather coat, hat, one gauntlet glove |
| *Warwick soldier*: | Dark grey tunic and helmet |
| *York soldier*: | Light grey tunic and helmet |
| *Mob*: | Grey gown, green-brown overgown, hat, belt with pouch |
| *Storm Trooper*: | Black padded tunic, lump belt, armband, heel tips, helmet with chain, gloves |
| *Executioner*: | Black apron, black tunic, black boots, black wrist bands, black tights, black helmet |
| *Gaoler*: | Camail, felt tabard, wide belt |
| *Abbey soldier*: | Blue-red tabard, camail, metal collar |
| *Citizen*: | Grey-white gown, brown cloak, fawn hood, leather hat, leather belt, tights, boots |

**BRIAN HARRISON**

| | |
|---|---|
| *Basic*: | Grey noile with chain sleeves |
| *French soldier*: | Orange-brown tunic and helmet |
| *Mob*: | Off-white shirt, black over-gown, studded belt |
| *York soldier*: | Light grey tunic and helmet |
| *Tyrrell*: | Black boots, shirt with chain arms, chain skirt, green tabard, belt, helmet with spurts, heel tips, gloves, gauntlets, armband |
| *Courtier*: | Lame shirt, green jacket with hanging sleeves, small belt, tights, boots |
| *Lancastrian soldier*: | Red tunic and helmet |

**IAN HOLM**

| | |
|---|---|
| *Richard*: | Chain legs, noile undershirt, brown jacket with calico bell sleeves, leather belt, calico brown jacket with long hanging sleeves, black |

and gold undershirt, chain of office, brown brocade jacket with hanging sleeves, belt, ring, red-brown gown and hat, monk's shirt, black jacket, belt, chain of office, short gold cloak, chain shirt and chain skirt, noile shirt with chain sleeves, ringed skirt, black armour, tabard, helmet with chain, right black leather glove, chain arm, chain collar, black legs, right arm, ball and chain, three crowns, floor cloth jacket with long hanging sleeves, silver armour right leg and arm, Coronation cloak

**JAMES HUNTER**

| | |
|---|---|
| *Basic*: | Grey noile with chain sleeves |
| *Young Talbot*: | Armour legs and arms, khaki leather tunic, helmet, gloves, lump belt |
| *French soldier*: | Orange-brown tunic and helmet |
| *Prince Edward*: | Red lame shirt, white jacket, belt, white gloves, red tights, boots, crown, grey gown, white tabard, armour legs and arms, belt, |
| helmet, | gloves |
| *Mob*: | Basic and brown cloak with hood, belt, hat |
| *Citizen*: | Short jacket, brown cloak, belt, hat |
| *Cleric*: | White underdress, gold cloak, white gloves, Mitre |
| *Burgundian soldier*: | Purple tunic, helmet with camail and blue flash |

**JOHN HUSSEY**

| | |
|---|---|
| *Somerset*: | Red lurex undershirt, red jacket, belt, red gown, red hat, gloves, red tabard, belt, armour legs and arms, helmet, gloves, gauntlets, chain of office, coronet, Coronation gown |
| *Ratcliffe*: | Noile underbodice garment, tabard, black stormtrooper jacket, armour legs, spurs, gauntlets, black suede gloves, ring, helmet, heel tips, Coronation gown, coronet, belt |

**BRIAN JACKSON**

| | |
|---|---|
| *Basic*: | Grey noile with chain sleeves |
| *Mob*: | Short boots, tie shirt, belt |
| *First Citizen*: | As Mob |
| *Holland*: | Long boots, grey tights, rags, tie, shirt, flecked smock, leather apron |
| *Ambassador*: | Blue-black velvet gown, hat, gloves, belt |

*Second Citizen -*
*Richard III* Gown, Frilled shirt, coat, hat, chain of office, belt, pouch
*Alderman*: Fur coat, chain of office

**MARTIN JENKINS**

*Basic*: Grey noile with chain sleeves
*Lancastrian soldier*: Red tunic and helmet
*Doctor*: Black gown and hat
*York soldier*: Light grey tunic and helmet
*Mob*: Ginger gown, hood, boots, belt, hat
*Vernon*: York tunic, hat, grey gown

**ROBERT JENNINGS**

*Basic*: Grey noile with chain sleeves
*Lancastrian soldier*: Red tunic and helmet
*York Irish*: Brown suede tunic with chain skirt attached, Metal helmet, collar
*York soldier*: Light grey tunic and helmet
*Citizen*: Black smock, belt, light green gown, hat
*Tower keeper*: Leather jacket, green cloak, hat, gloves, belt
*Mob*: As Citizen with brown tabard, brown hat

**MARSHALL JONES**

*Basic*: Grey noile with chain sleeves
*Weaver*: Short grey boots, brown gown, leather tabard, apron, belt, grey hood
*Lancastrian soldier*: Red tunic and helmet
*York soldier*: Light grey tunic and helmet
*Mob*: Dark grey smock with brown sleeves, leather tabard, belt, hood, red hat
*Storm Trooper*: Black padded tunic, heel tips, armband, leather tabard, helmet, gloves, belt
*Talbot soldier*: Khaki tunic, helmet with camail and orange flash
*Abbey soldier*: Blue-red tabard, camail
*Citizen*: Under shirt, blue-grey long gown, belt, overgown, chain of office, black gloves, pointed grey hat
*Alderman*: Fur collared gown, chain of office, hat

**ROGER JONES**

| | |
|---|---|
| *Basic*: | Grey noile with chain sleeves |
| *York soldier*: | Light grey tunic and helmet |
| *Talbot soldier*: | Khaki tunic, helmet with camail and orange flash |
| *Falconer*: | Feather coat, hat, one gauntlet glove |
| *Mob*: | Leather jerkin (York Irish), Cloak, hat |
| *York Irish*: | Leather jerkin, tin helmet, tin collar |
| *Lancastrian soldier*: | Red tunic and helmet |
| *Storm Trooper*: | Black padded tunic, heel tips, helmet, belt, chain gloves, armband, Monk's hood for Richard III |

**CHARLES KAY**

| | |
|---|---|
| *Hume*: | Grey wool undergown, dark red-purple overgown, cowl, boots, belt with keys, purse, inkwell, cross and chain, mittens |
| *Clarence*: | Brown floorcloth jacket, leather belt, chain tights, armour legs and arms, front tabard, belt cloak, helmet, gloves, back tabard, brown-gold shirt, brown jacket with hanging sleeves, chain of office, gloves, chain gloves, sandals, large belt with sword, ghost shirt, lighter brown shirt, opulent shirt |

**HENRY KNOWLES**

| | |
|---|---|
| *Basic*: | Grey noile with chain sleeves |
| *Lancastrian soldier*: | Red tunic, helmet and belt |
| *York soldier*: | Light grey tunic, helmet |
| *York Irish:* | Leather jerkin, breast plate, helmet |
| *Burgundian soldier*: | Purple tunic, helmet with camail and blue flash |
| *French soldier*: | Orange-brown tunic, helmet |
| *Storm Trooper*: | Black padded tunic, heel tips, helmet, belt, gloves, armband |
| *Mob*: | Green dress, dark green tabard, belt, cowl |
| *Cleric*: | White underdress, white and gold cloak, white gloves, mitre, white collar |
| *Courtier*: | Green and gold shirt, green tunic, gold belt, boots, tights, hat |
| *York Messenger*: | Grey cloak |

**ROY MARSDEN**

| | |
|---|---|
| *Basic*: | Grey noile with chain sleeves |
| *Lancastrian soldier*: | Red tunic, helmet |

| | |
|---|---|
| *French soldier*: | Orange-brown tunic and helmet |
| *York soldier*: | Light grey tunic, helmet |
| *York Irish*: | Leather jerkin, fur shoulders, helmet, metal collar |
| *Mob*: | Oatmeal undergarment, belt, ginger brown boots |
| *Rivers*: | Gold jacket, gold belt, tights, boots, hat, gloves, gown, gold tabard, armour legs and arms, helmet with chain, gloves, belt, sandals, chain of office, shift |

**BREWSTER MASON**

| | |
|---|---|
| *Warwick*: | Brown and gold shirt, belt for boots, grey jacket, heavy belt, dagger, gloves, armour legs and arms, tabard, helmet, belt, collar, brown hat, cloak, silver gown, under bodice, bloody tabard, armour gloves |

**RHYS McCONNOCHIE**

| | |
|---|---|
| *Basic*: | Grey noile with chain sleeves |
| *Lancastrian soldier*: | Red tunic and helmet |
| *York soldier*: | Light grey tunic and helmet |
| *Mob*: | Green smock, brown leather jacket, brown hood, black hat |
| *Alencon*: | Blue jacket, hat, boots, armour legs, belt, night-shirt, shawl, chain shirt |
| *Breton officer*: | Boots, belt, helmet, brown leather tabard, cloak |
| *Storm trooper*: | Black padded tunic, heel tips, belt, armband, gloves, helmet |

**IAN McCULLOCH**

| | |
|---|---|
| *Basic*: | Grey noile with chain sleeves |
| *Lancastrian soldier*: | Red tunic and helmet |
| *York soldier*: | Light grey tunic and helmet |
| *French soldier*: | Orange-blue tunic, helmet |
| *Mob*: | Straw hat, smock, scarf, leather belt, boots |
| *Catesby*: | Boots, tights, black-silver shirt, green jacket with hanging sleeves, chain gloves, green cloak, armour legs, chain underbodice, dark green tabard, spurs, leather boots, belt, gauntlets, helmet, heel tips, armour belt, Coronation gown, coronet |

**MICHAEL MURRAY**

| | |
|---|---|
| *Papal legate*: | White gown, black overgown, large red hat, leather belt, gloves |
| *Oxford*: | Red shirt, dark grey tunic, belt, gauntlet gloves, grey gown, noile underbodice, grey tabard, armour arms and legs, helmet with chain, chain of office, armour belt, gloves, red gown |

**TIM NIGHTINGALE**

| | |
|---|---|
| *Basic*: | Grey noile with chain sleeves |
| *York soldier*: | Light grey tunic and helmet |
| *Warwick soldier*: | Dark grey tunic and helmet |
| *Gaoler*: | Felt tabard, camail, belt |
| *Falconer*: | Feathery coat and hat, one gauntlet glove |
| *Storm trooper*: | Black padded tunic, heel tips, belt, armband, helmet, chain gloves |
| *Abbey soldier*: | Blue-red tabard, metal collar, camail |

**JOHN NORMINGTON**

| | |
|---|---|
| *Clifford*: | Red tunic, belt, gloves, red cloak, red tabard, armour legs and arms, helmet, gloves, belt, chain of office |
| *Old Mortimer*: | White night shirt, dark green dressing gown |
| *Simpcox*: | Grey trousers, bandages, tattered shirt, socks, woolly vest, string coat, white bandage, begging cup |
| *Lord Citizen*: | White shirt with frill, green gown with velvet sleeves, chain attached, red-brown cloak, hat, little hat |
| *Alderman*: | Fur cloak, jewelled hat, chain of office |

**CLIFFORD ROSE**

| | |
|---|---|
| *Exeter*: | Grey jacket, belt, hat, grey gown, tabard, armour legs and arms, helmet with chain, gloves, coronet, black padding, belt for boots |
| *First Murderer*: | Boots, black jacket, belt, dagger, black overjerkin, pouch, gloves, belt for boots |

**DAVID ROWLAND**

| | |
|---|---|
| *Basic*: | Grey noile with chain sleeves |
| *Talbot soldier*: | Khaki tunic, helmet with camail and orange flash |
| *York soldier*: | Light grey tunic and helmet |
| *York Irish*: | Leather jacket, York helmet, metal collar |

| | |
|---|---|
| *Mob*: | Grey-blue shirt, belt, black hat |
| *Storm Trooper*: | Black padded tunic, belt, heel tips, gloves, armband, helmet |
| *Abbey soldier*: | Blue-red tabard, collar, camail |

**NICHOLAS SELBY**

| | |
|---|---|
| *Winchester*: | White shirt, gold gown, gold-white cope, stole, mitre, gloves, green dress, red cloak attached, red gloves, red hat, cross and chain, leather belt, green dress, red cloak, square hat, round red hat, two red rings, silk cape, death hat, hood, death gloves |
| *Father who killed son*: | York tunic, camail |

**DONALD SINDEN**

| | |
|---|---|
| *York*: | Grey jacket, belt, chain of office, grey gown, hat, lamé underbodice, grey tabard, armour legs and arms, chain collar, helmet, belt, gloves, bloody tabard, gauntlets, light grey jacket, noile underbodice, coronet, Coronation gown |

**DEREK SMITH**

| | |
|---|---|
| *Talbot*: | Black underbodice, with chain attached, khaki leather tunic, armour legs and arms, helmet with chain, chain gloves, lump belt, coronet |
| *Jack Cade*: | Khaki tights, shirt, chain mail collar, brown leather jerkin, belt, leather gloves, extra leather belt |

**JOHN STEINER**

| | |
|---|---|
| *Basic*: | Grey noile with chain sleeves |
| *Talbot soldier*: | Khaki tunic, helmet with camail with orange flash |
| *York soldier*: | Light grey tunic and helmet |
| *Warwick soldier*: | Dark grey tunic and helmet |
| *Mob*: | Grey gown with light sleeves, leather jerkin, cloak, belt, fur hat |
| *Abbey soldier*: | Red-blue tabard with metal collar, camail |
| *Breton Officer*: | Brown leather tunic, belt, cloak, helmet with chain |
| *Tressel*: | Black coat, hat, belt, black gloves |

**HUGH SULLIVAN**

| | |
|---|---|
| *Orleans*: | Brown-green jacket with knitted collar, chain gloves, hat, night shirt, armour legs, belt, helmet |
| *Iden*: | Leather belt with sword, off-white gown, gloves, grey hat |
| *Hastings*: | Brown lamé shirt, green jacket with bell sleeves, green gown, belt, ghost shirt, chain of office, long gown, nightdress, dress belt, hat, green tabard, underbodice, armour legs and arms, cloak, hat, shirt and trousers |

**DAVID WALSH**

| | |
|---|---|
| *Basic*: | Grey noile with chain sleeves |
| *York soldier*: | Light grey tunic and helmet |
| *Lancastrian soldier*: | Red tunic, helmet |
| *Abbey soldier*: | Blue-red tabard, belt, collar, camail |
| *Falconer*: | Feathery coat and hat, one gauntlet glove |
| *Talbot soldier*: | Khaki tunic, helmet with camail and orange flash |
| *Storm trooper*: | Black padded tunic, belt, armband, chain gloves, helmet, heel tips |
| *Doctor*: | Black gown with white collar, black hat |
| *Citizen*: | Light green smock with dark green collar, belt, black hat |
| *Warwick soldier*: | Dark grey tunic and helmet |
| *Mob*: | Grey undershirt, black flecked smock, leather jerkin |
| | Three purses |

**DAVID WARNER**

| | |
|---|---|
| *Henry*: | Grey gown, grey cloak, metal collar, gloves, grey hat, Coronation cloak, Coronation gown, ragged gown, ghost outfit, one gownless evening strap, two small lump belts, sword belt, chain gauntlets, rosary, off-white shift (to wear in coffin) |

**DEREK WARING**

| | |
|---|---|
| *Dauphin*: | Blue-gold jacket with small cape, sword belt, hat, gauntlets,boots, copper armour legs, one slipper, night shirt, armour gloves |
| *King of France*: | Blue-gold gown, lump belt, boots, crown, padding, chain of office |
| *Richmond*: | Leather jacket, belt, sword, boots, tabard, armour legs, chain collar, chain tights, brown cloak |

**JOHN WELSH**

| | |
|---|---|
| *Gloucester*: | Black gown, black and red cloak, gloves, hat, coronet, black under bodice, belt, night shirt, chain of office, riding whip |

**TIM WYLTON**

| | |
|---|---|
| *Basic*: | Grey noile with chain sleeves |
| *Lancastrian soldier*: | Red tunic and helmet |
| *York soldier*: | Light grey tunic and helmet |
| *Mob*: | Oatmeal jacket, gown with fur collar, black hat |
| *Talbot soldier*: | Khaki tunic, helmet with camail and orange flash |
| *York Irish*: | Red costume with leather collar, York helmet |
| *Michael*: | Leather jerkin, grey-green shirt, belt, grey hood, dagger |

**KEN WYNNE**

| | |
|---|---|
| *Bolingbroke*: | Boots, tatty trousers, jacket with cloak attached, belt with pouch and charms, hat |
| *Lord Say*: | Dark green jacket, grey-green gown, belt, boots, chain of office |

# INDEX

## BIBLIOGRAPHY

*David Addenbrooke:* The Royal Shakespeare Company - The Peter Hall Years. William Kimber. 1974.

*C.T. Allmand:* Shakespeare's Version of the Age. History of the English Speaking Peoples Volume 3. New Caxton Library. 1969.

*Dame Peggy Ashcroft:* Margaret of Anjou. Deutsche Shakespeare - Gesellschaft West Jahrbuch. 1974.

*John Barton and Peter Hall:* The Wars of the Roses. BBC. 1970.

*Sally Beauman:* The Royal Shakespeare Company: A History in Ten Decades.
Oxford at the University Press. 1982.

*Michael Billington:* Peggy Ashcroft. John Murray. 1988.

*Peter Brook:* The Empty Space. Penguin. 1968.

*John Russell Brown:* Shakespeare's Plays in Performance. Penguin. 1967.

*Michael L. Greenwald:* Directions by Indirections. University of Delaware. 1985.

*John Bury:* Against Falsehood. RSC Flourish Newspaper. 1965.

*Julie Hankey:* Richard III. Plays in Performance. Junction Books. 1981.

*Holly Hill:* Playing Joan. Theatre Communications Group Inc. 1987.

*Barbara Hodgson:* The Wars of the Roses: Scholarship speaks on stage. Deutsche Shakespeare - Gesellschaft West Jahrbuch. 1972.

*Jan Kott:* Shakespeare Our Contemporary. Methuen. 1965.

*Robert Potter:* The Rediscovery of Queen Margaret: The Wars of the Roses. 1963.

*Riverside Shakespeare:* Houghton Miflin Company. 1974.

*Royal Shakespeare Company:* Crucial Years. Max Reinhardt. 1963.

*Donald Sinden:* Laughter in the Second Act. Hodder and Stoughton. 1986.